My First Model United Nations Conference

Demystifying Model UN, One Conference at a Time

Vivian Armitage

My First Model UN Conference

©2016 by Vivian Armitage

Cover Design: Jonna Feavel

40daygraphics.com

Interior Layout: Daniel Mawhinney

40daypublishing.com

Also available in eBook publication

Printed in the United States of America

FOR ALL THE MODEL UN DELEGATES OUT THERE;

KEEP RESEARCHING, DEBATING, AND COLLABORATING.

Contents

Author's Introduction

First of all, hello! Thank you for picking up my book. I am excited to act as your guide on the journey that will lead you to your first Model United Nations conference. I am sure you are curious about every aspect of the process and have a ton of questions about what it takes to partake in Model UN. Well, prepare to learn the ins-and-outs of preparation, participation, and parliamentary procedure. What is parliamentary procedure, you ask? Have no fear, by the end of this book you will not only understand parliamentary procedure, you will be a pro at rising on points of personal privilege, yielding time to the chair, and motioning to move into voting procedure.

Model UN will change your life. By embracing this phenomenal opportunity, you will gain relevant experience, applicable knowledge, and a newfound understanding of the world. So, accept the challenge. Participate in a conference. It will be one of the best decisions you will ever make. Acting as a delegate will force you to hone your writing and public speaking skills, enhance your knowledge of current events, and most importantly, broaden your horizons. Engaging in this experience will equip you with the tools necessary to resolve the problems facing the world. You will become a catalyst of change. If you welcome the test, embrace new opinions, and apply your knowledge to relevant situations, you will be well on your way to assuming a prestigious leadership role.

"You must be the change you wish to see in the world."

-Mahatma Ghandi

I hope you will find this book comprehensive, interesting, and informative. I am encouraged by your desire to better yourself, and your community, by participating in the positive experience that is Model UN. After this event, you will be a leader, luminary, and lexicon of knowledge, whose knowledge of global issues, ability to resolve conflict, and determination to improve the lives of others will uplift the world. I am confidant that with your help, we will make the Earth a better place to live. Now, prepare yourself for the challenges to come and embark on your journey. Your whole life has been building to this moment. I trust you will seize this opportunity to improve yourself and inspire others to join your cause along the way.

Best of luck,

Vivian B. Armitage

My Story

My name is Vivian Armitage. I am a high school student and I live in Oklahoma City. When I attended my first Model UN conference, I was a shy sixth grader who hated public speaking. As a novice delegate, my mom, brother, and I flew to Washington, D.C. to participate in a Model UN training session. However, I was not excited to participate in the conference. At the sessions, I was nervous, uncomfortable, and alone. I dealt with my fear by walking to the different informational sessions with a grim look on my face and taking aggressive notes, so I wouldn't have to interact with anyone. I didn't say a word at that conference. Despite all of my note-taking, I couldn't gather the courage to participate. I was so intimidated by parliamentary procedure that I missed the opportunity to collaborate with the delegates in my committee. In hindsight, I wish I had spoken up.

While my first encounter with Model UN was intimidating, I decided to attend another conference, and I am so glad I did.

Model UN has been an invaluable experience for me. Not only has it taught me about the world, international relations, and the benefits of collaboration; it has forced me to step out of my comfort zone, which has been both the most challenging, and most rewarding lesson of all.

Now, over six years later, I have represented a variety of countries at multiple conferences, including Harvard and Georgetown. As a seasoned delegate, I now understand the ins and outs of Model UN, and most importantly, I finally understand how to ask the Chair to turn the air conditioning up while using proper parliamentary procedure.

Currently, I am the president of the Model United Nations club at my school, and a voracious writer. I wrote a curriculum for a Model UN workshop designed to instruct middle school students on how to effectively participate in a conference. I have presented this "Done in a Day" curriculum at the University of Oklahoma for two years.

Although I finally have the knowledge and courage to be an active participant in Model UN conferences, I am still not satisfied. I want to make sure other students are not scared off by Model UN. I want to ensure that no one else feels the way I did at my first conference. I want you to be a poised and confident delegate with an understanding of parliamentary procedure, even if you don't completely understand it, which practically no one does.

My mission is to spread the benefits of Model UN to students around the world. I hope that by introducing students to Model UN and teaching them how to participate in a conference, a new generation of engaged global citizens will emerge.

What is the United Nations?

If you have heard of the United Nations, you are well ahead of where I was seven years ago. However, if your only knowledge of this entity is its name, or you suspect it has something to do with a group of countries, or you have no idea what the United Nations is; have no fear! This chapter will cover the world-wide phenomenon that is the United Nations. And no matter the depth of your present understanding of this institution, with any luck, by the end of this chapter you will at least learn something new about this behemoth of an organization.

The United Nations was founded on October 24, 1945, and replaced the unsuccessful League of Nations which had been created at the end of the First World War. Since its founding at the conclusion of World War II, the United Nations has quickly become the largest and most influential non-governmental body in the international community.

Currently, there are 193 countries that serve as member states of the United Nations. The United Nations has six official languages: Arabic, Chinese, English, French, Russian, and Spanish. The United Nations has its own flag, post office, and postage stamps. The United Nations is headquartered in New York City, but the land the building occupies is recognized as international territory. Additionally, the United Nations has offices in Vienna, Austria; Addis Ababa, Ethiopia; Amman, Jordan; Bangkok, Thailand; and Santiago, Chile.

As a unique international organization, the United Nations can take action on the variety of issues that face the global community. Some of the issues the organization has worked to resolve include: climate change, disasters and emergencies, terrorism, gender equality, the spread of infectious diseases, peace and security, human rights, and nuclear disarmament.

Not only does the United Nations serve as an agent of change in the international community, but it also provides member states the opportunity to voice their opinions in a forum setting, providing countries the ability to collaborate, build relationships, and resolve global issues.

The United Nations is divided into five principal organs:

- Economic and Social Council
- General Assembly
- International Court of Justice
- Secretariat
- Security Council

Each of these entities address relevant concerns, resolve international problems, and aim to improve the state of the world.

The Economic and Social Council (ECOSOC) is responsible for championing innovative development goals with an emphasis on economic, environmental, and social issues. ECOSOC has 65 members, and holds one week-long meeting each July. The members are selected by the General Assembly based on geographical representation: eighteen seats from African states, thirteen seats for Asian states, eight seats for East European states, thirteen seats for Latin American and Caribbean states, and thirteen seats for West European states. Member states serve three-year terms. Resolutions enacted by ECOSOC do not become international law, but are merely suggested action steps for the General Assembly to consider. Participating in an ECOSOC committee provides a delegate with a smaller, more focused experience, and would be beneficial for students who are interested in economic, social, or environmental issues.

The General Assembly (GA) is the main body of the United Nations. Each member state is represented in this committee. The GA sets the standards of the United Nations as an entity, and codifies the majority of international law. Member states are awarded one vote each, and the GA requires a two-thirds majority to pass substantive resolutions. A simple majority is required for all other non-substantive resolutions. The GA provides all countries with an equal opportunity to participate. Since, the GA is the largest and most inclusive body, it is often the best place for novice delegates to begin.

The International Court of Justice (ICJ) handles all legal queries, and advises the United Nations on legal issues. Fifteen judges compose the ICJ. These judges elected by the General Assembly and the Security Council and serve nine year terms. The ICJ does not operate like most other committees, but runs similarly to a court trial. Delegates who participate in the ICJ serve as a judge on a prosecution or defense team, or as a witness. Additionally, preparation is extremely important in this committee. While delegates who participate in the ICJ will not experience a typical Model UN committee, they will be exposed to the world of international law and learn the ins-and-outs of litigation. Students who wish to pursue legal careers should consider this committee.

The Secretariat is responsible for setting the agenda for the other four bodies of the UN and enforcing said decisions in each principal organ. The Secretariat is staffed by nationals of member states. The head of the Secretariat, who is appointed by the General Assembly, is the Secretary General. The Secretariat is in charge of a variety of committees and organizations that serve as subsidiaries of the United Nations. In Model UN, the Secretariat consists of the group of students or teachers who organize and run the conference.

The Security Council (UNSC) is responsible for maintaining international peace and ensuring global security. Of all the principal organs, the UNSC is the most powerful. Fifteen member nations compose the UNSC: five permanent members, and ten elected members. The permanent member states, who have veto power, are: China, France, Russian Federation, United Kingdom, and United States. The elected members serve two-year terms, and are not granted the same level of gravitas as the permanent members. A UNSC committee in a Model UN conference tends to be intense, concentrated, and and overall stimulating experience. It is unlikely that a novice delegate will participate on the UNSC.

In addition to the main organs, the United Nations has a variety of specialized committees and subsidiary organizations that focus on specific global issues. Some of these committees include: International Monetary Fund (IMF), United Nations Children's Fund (UNICEF), United Nations Office on Drugs and Crime (UNODC), World Food Programme (WFP), and World Health Organization (WHO.)

Today, the United Nations is the world's most important agency for keeping peace. For over seventy years, it has facilitated discussion, promoted conflict resolution, and improve the global community. Without the United Nations, the citizens would not enjoy the same luxuries, nor would we experience the same level of order and concord. The United Nations has transformed the world we live in, improving education, expanding medical care, and increasing environmental protection. Its ambassadors have assumed the challenging roles of intermediary, and have acted on behalf of their citizens to improve the human experience. Overall, the United Nations is an all-around amazing organization, and we, as global citizens, should be eternally grateful for their valiant efforts and indefatigable service.

What is Model United Nations?

As you gaze down at this page, I am sure most of you are thinking one or all of these questions: what is Model United Nations, what happens at a conference, who participates in Model United Nations, and why should I participate in Model United Nations.

Now, by the end of this book, I hope I will have answered these questions, and more. But for now, I will address the first: what is Model United Nations, or Model UN?

Model United Nations is an academic exercise where students attend committee sessions authentic to the United Nations, such as the General Assembly and Security Council. The goal of Model UN is to introduce students to international issues, sharpen their negotiation skills, and promote delegate collaboration.

Before attending a Model UN conference and assuming an ambassadorial role, delegates research the topic area that will be debated in committee. Prior to the conference, delegates educate themselves on the issue as a whole, their country's position and involvement, and the steps that have been taken to resolve the problem. The topic areas which students discuss in committee are vast, with issues ranging from human rights, to environmental protection, to economic development, to global health concerns, to globalization.

Most Model UN conferences are offered to students at the middle school, high school, and collegiate level, but a few conferences are held exclusively for elementary school students.

During a Model UN conference, students assume the role of an ambassador, and represent the views of one of the 193 United Nations member states. Delegates debate current global issues using parliamentary procedure, propose practical solutions, craft draft resolutions, and collaborate with other countries in an effort to solve problems facing the international community.

Unlike most academic competitions, the purpose of participating in a Model UN conference is not to win an award. While delegates can receive awards at a Model UN conference, the promise of a trophy is not the chief reason students partake in this exercise. Model UN conferences are far more evolved. Instead of striving to beat other students in the hopes of being awarded a first place trophy, Model UN delegates encourage each other and focus on collaboration rather than competition. Furthermore, when being assessed for an award, students are judged on their ability to communicate, compromise, and cooperate with other countries rather than their personal skills or individual achievements.

By participating in a conference, students will learn the value of team-work and correspondence when faced with a pervasive issue. These and other skills will provide you with the tools you need to become an informed, engaged, and effective global citizen.

Now, for those of you who learn better through lists, bullet points, or outlines, I have you covered! Here are some of the skills you will develop by participating in a Model UN conference:

- Research
- Public Speaking
- Writing
- Critical Thinking
- Debate
- Listening
- Leadership
- Collaboration
- Negotiation
- Compromise

Why Participate in Model UN?

Many of you may be thinking, "Sure it is great to learn about research, public speaking, and collaboration before I become an adult, but why should I spend my weekend finding facts on an obscure country, or writing a formated paper when I could be binge watching Netflix and eating raw cookie dough, instead."

Well, while lounging in one's pajamas and vegging-out in front of the television does sound like an enjoyable way to spend a Saturday, the reparation for recusing oneself from the world for twelve hours is not nearly as high as the reward of partaking in an engaging and educational simulation.

If that did not convince you that Model UN is a worthy way to spend your time, here is a list of reasons why attending a conference will provide an invaluable experience, enrich your life, and broaden your horizons.

First of all, participating in conferences is a great way to meet people; meaning it is a great way to make new friends you wouldn't have the opportunity to meet otherwise.

Secondly, participating in Model UN is great for building public speaking skills, which are important to develop as you move into high school and college. Third of all, you get to learn about current events, which makes you an engaged citizen, and also means you can show off your knowledge to parents, friends, teachers, and the like. And finally, practicing parliamentary procedure and learning about Model UN will provide insight into the workings of the United Nations, the most relevant international, peacekeeping agency.

Still not sold on Model UN? What if I told you that Model UN would get you into the college of your choice. Do I have your attention now? Good. When college admissions officers see the words 'Model UN' on a resume, they immediately associate you with one of these traits, or a similar characteristic: intelligent, worldly, engaged, or inclusive. Honestly, how could they not? Model UN tells people you have never met that you would be a valuable addition to any program you wish to attend, campus you aspire to live on, or position you desire to hold. Not only does Model UN serve as a valuable addition to a resume, it can be the key to paying for college. Every year, scholarships are given to outstanding Model UN delegates who desire to continue their education at university. Not a bad deal for participating in such an enjoyable activity. So, if you attend a conference, learn the ins-and-outs of debate, and hone your speaking skills, these financial packages could be yours, too.

Hopefully, if you were not interested in Model UN before you opened this book, you are eager to dive into the nitty-gritty of research and parliamentary procedure. No matter your excitement level, if you have any interest in Model UN at all, please give it a chance. Attend a conference; the experience might surprise you.

Again, for those of you 'organizational learners,' here is a list of the wonderful things Model UN imparts upon students just like you. Participating in a conference will...

- teach you about current events.

- increase your understanding of international politics.

- make you a more engaged world citizen.

- widen your horizons.

- allow you to understand parliamentary procedure.

- enhance your writing style.

- improve your public speaking skills.

- provide you the opportunity to meet fun, engaged, like-mind people like yourself.

- supply you with otherwise unattainable opportunities.

- prove advantageous resume fodder.

- equip you with the skills necessary to function as a member of the ever-changing global community.

How to Start a Model UN Club at Your School

So, you want to start a Model UN club at your school. You have been bitten by the MUN bug, and you want to share your passion with your classmates, teachers, and community at large. The only problem is, you have no idea where to begin. Fortunately for you, starting a Model UN club is not as hard as you might expect. If you follow these simple guidelines, you will be one step closer to your dream of changing the world.

1.   Get permission. Most schools have requirements for establishing clubs. Meet with an administrator, teacher, or supervisor before you begin the process to ensure you are in accordance with the rules and requirements.

2.   Identify a faculty advisor. Once you have learned the qualifications for creating a new organization at your school, approach your favorite teacher, counselor, or mentor and ask them if they would be interested in supervising your club. History, english, and language teachers tend to exhibit the most interest in Model UN, but that is not to say that your math teacher would not be interested in filling the role.

3.   Find a meeting place. Whether it is in a classroom, at the library, or at your house, you need to establish a location for your club to assemble and discuss conference details.

4.   Establish a meeting time. Review your schedule and decide the best date and time for your club to meet. Thursday at 3:30 works for you? Perfect! Pencil the recurring event into your calendar, and write the information on your flyer.

5.   Write a curriculum for your club. Your agenda can be a simple one-page list of meeting dates and topics, or it could be a thick binder with activities, exercises, and videos for each meeting. No matter how detailed you want your curriculum be, be sure you have some semblance of a schedule. Otherwise your club meetings will digress into discussions of Keeping Up With the Kardashians, or you could find yourself going on coffee runs when you should be learning parliamentary procedure.

6.   Set a goal. You want to attend the Harvard Model United Nations Conference this year? Go for it! Making concrete goals is a great way to inspire students to join your club. Not to mention that it is a wonderful motivational tool when you are feeling less than inspired to start your position paper.

7.   Make flyers. How will students know about your club if you do not advertise your awesomeness? Be sure you include: what the club is about, what you will learn by participating, meeting time, length of meeting, meeting location, cost, who is eligible to join, and your contact information. Additionally, embellishments such as fun graphics, pictures, or maps can enhance your message and draw more eyes to your poster.

8.   Establish a communication network. Take down contact information from each student who attends your first club meeting. This will be helpful when you send out surveys, or if you need to send a group message.

9.   Start a social media page. Have fun with your club! Start a Facebook, Instagram, or Twitter account to share information and inspiration with other clubs, and to connect with other devoted MUNers just like yourself.

10.   Have officer elections. Vote on Secretary-General, Rapporteur and Treasurer of the club. Creating engaging leadership positions is a great way to get students involved in your club, and a surreptitious way to delegate responsibilities that tend to be less than exciting. Who really wants to be responsible for receipts anyway?

11.   Register for a conference. After all, this is the reason you started a club. No matter how big or small your first conference is, bring an enthusiastic delegation, and prepare to learn a lot.

12.   Fundraise. Although not every club has a bank account, it might be a good idea to start raising money for your next trip. Who knows, maybe you will raise enough money that you can establish a scholarship for students interested in Model UN who would otherwise be unable to attend a conference. Hold a bake sale, have a car wash, or just ask parents, teachers, or administrators for sponsorships.

13.   Begin preparing for your conference! Now that you have created a new club, and gathered a few members, it is time to hit the ground running and being the journey to your first MUN conference. Let the planning begin!

Nice work! You just pioneered your own club. Pat yourself on the back. That is not to say your task is complete. Far from finished, actually. If anything, the work is just beginning. That is a discussion for a different time, however, for now just focus on encouraging your club members and begin looking for a conference. Still do not know where to begin? No worries, we will walk you through each step of Model UN preparation. In no time you will be a parliamentary procedure pro, the first delegate on the Speaker's List, and an accomplished resolution author. Don't know what any of that means? Then we better get started.

Basic 1 Day Model UN Conference Schedule

8:00 am- Check-in begins

9:00 am- Welcome and Introduction

9:30 am- First committee session begins

12 noon- Lunch Break/time to work on resolutions

1 pm- Second committee session begins

3:30 pm- Break/time to work on resolutions

4:00 pm- Third committee session begins

6:30 pm- Dinner Break

7:30 pm- Awards ceremony

8:00 pm- Closing remarks and conference adjournment

~This is merely an example of a conference schedule, many conferences end before dinner or earlier in the day~

Basic Long-Weekend Model UN Conference Schedule

Day 1:

8:00 am- Check-in begins

9:00 am- Welcome and Introduction

9:30 am- First committee session begins

12 noon- Lunch Break

1:30 pm- Second committee session begins

6:00 pm- Dinner Break

8:00 pm- Third committee session begins

10:00 pm- Recess

Day 2:

9:00am- Fourth committee session begins

12 noon- Lunch Break and Free Time

3:00 pm- Fifth committee session begins

6:00 pm- Dinner Break

8:00 pm- Sixth committee session begins

10:00 pm- Recess

Day 3:

9:00 am- Seventh committee session begins

12 noon- Lunch Break

1:30- Eighth committee session begins

4:00- Awards and Closing Ceremony

Basic Model UN Terms

Adjourn: A vote of adjournment suspends debate until the next meeting, whether the meeting is the next day or the next year. No matter the timeline, each Model UN conference concludes with a vote of adjournment.

Agenda: The agenda is the schedule of the committee session. This determines the order in which the topic areas will be discussed.

Amendment: An amendment alters the structure of a draft resolution. The proposed change can be small, like a grammatical correction, or large, like the addition of a clause. No matter how dramatic the alteration is, amendments fall into two categories: friendly and unfriendly.

Bloc: A group of countries with similar views on a topic, or a coalition of countries from the same area of the world (i.e. Middle Eastern or African countries.)

Chair: The member of the dias who enforces parliamentary procedure, moderates debate, keeps time, and rules on points and motions. The Chair is also referred to as the Moderator.

Dias: The group of students or teachers who lead and regulate a committee session. These members include: the Chair, the Director, and the Rapporteur.

Decorum: The composure each Model UN delegate must maintain. This includes respecting the Dias, their fellow delegates, and the country they represent. Decorum is basically a set of manners each delegate is required to practice during committee.

Delegate: A student acting as a representative from one of the 193 member states of the United Nations.

Delegation: A group of students who represent one of the United Nations member states. Usually, one school represents one delegation.

Draft Resolution: A document that aims to resolve a specific issue facing the global community. Draft resolutions are crafted by a bloc of delegates known as sponsors; if passed by the committee, a draft resolution will become a resolution.

Friendly Amendment: An amendment to a draft resolution that is authored by the sponsors of said draft resolution. Once the amendment is approved by each sponsor and the Chair of the committee session, it will be adopted into the body of the resolution.

Gavel: The device by which the Chair keeps order in the committee. A gavel is shaped like a wooden hammer.

Lobbying: Unofficial, informal caucusing between delegates or delegations. Lobbying often occurs outside the committee room. Delegates frequently lobby to garner support on resolutions, or to encourage other delegations to vote for a specific topic area.

Member State: A country whose application to join the United Nations has been approved by the General Assembly and the Security Council. The country must also ratify and agree with the Charter of the United Nations. Currently, there are 193 member states.

Merging: When countries combine draft resolutions in order to make a larger, or more relevant resolution.

Moderated Caucus: A form of debate where the Chair facilitates the discussion. During a moderated caucus, delegates remain seated until the Chair recognizes them to speak. When motioning for a moderated caucus, a delegate must propose a time limit, specific topic to debate, and establish speaking time.

Motion: A request made by a single delegate that is relevant to the entire committee. Motions include: moderated caucus, unmoderated caucus, introduce draft resolutions, and move into voting procedure.

Page: A delegate who volunteers to pass notes to other delegates in committee. In Model UN, passing notes is not only allowed, it is encouraged.

Placard: A piece of paper embossed with a country's name. Placards are distributed to each delegate, and are used to get the Chair's attention, or to signal that a delegate wishes to speak.

Point: A request for information. Delegates can rise on a variety of points, including: point of information, point of order, and point of personal privilege.

Position Paper: A paper written prior to a conference that summarizes a delegate's position on the topic that is to be debated in committee.

Resolution: A document that outlines the necessary action steps the United Nations and its member states should taken in order to deal with a specific issue. A resolution begins as a working paper, then becomes a draft resolution; and finally, if the committee agrees with its content and provides a vote of approval, it becomes a resolution.

Right of Reply: A response to a speaker's comment, if said comment insults another country. A country may exercise this right in an attempt to defend the honor of its country. A delegate must ask the Chair for permission before rising on this point.

Roll Call: The first order of business in each committee session. During roll call, the Rapporteur will read the names of each member state. When a delegate's country's name is called, he or she may respond "present" or "present and voting." If a delegate responds "present and voting," he or she may not abstain on a substantive vote.

Second: Basically a point of approval. A second supports the claim or proposal of another delegate. Motions must be seconded before they can be voted upon.

Secretariat: The group of students or teachers who compose the staff of a Model UN conference.

Secretary-General: Similar to a class President, the secretary-general serves as the leader of a Model UN conference.

Signatory: A country that wants to see a draft resolution debated. A signatory is not required to support the draft resolution, but wants it to be added to the docket. Each conference requires each draft resolution to have a specific number of signatories before it can be discussed.

Simple Majority: A simple majority is 50% of the committee. Half of the delegates must be in favor of a proposal for most votes to be passed.

Speaker's List: A list that determines the order in which delegates will be recognized to speak on behalf of their country. When a speaker's list is introduced, delegates may be added to the list by raising their placards and being recognized by the Chair. Later in committee, a delegate may join the speaker's list by passing a note to the Dias.

Sponsor: A delegate who authors a draft resolution, or who collaborates with other delegates on creating a draft resolution.

Topic Area: The subject of debate. A topic area serves as the focus of the committee. Topic areas include: spread of infectious disease, international terrorism, nuclear proliferation, and organ trafficking.

Unfriendly Amendment: An amendment to a draft resolution that is proposed by a delegate who has not contributed to said draft resolution. The committee must vote upon each unfriendly amendment before it is added to a draft resolution. Unfriendly resolutions are voted upon before a draft resolution is approved.

Unmoderated Caucus: A caucus where delegates are allowed to leave their seats and speak without being recognized by the Chair. An unmoderated caucus provides delegates the ability to collaborate with other countries, from country blocs, and craft draft resolutions.

Vet: The ability of a select country to vote "no" and thereby prevent a draft resolution from being approved. This privilege is given to China, France, Great Britain, the Russian Federation, and the United States.

Vote: A time when delegates indicate their support for or opposition to an action proposed in committee. A vote falls into one of two categories: procedural or substantive.

Voting Procedure: The period at the end of a committee session when delegates vote on amendments and draft resolutions. Delegates are prohibited from both entering and leaving the room during voting procedure.

Working Paper: The first step to creating a resolution. Working papers express the actions a group of countries believe the committee should take to resolve a problem. Amendments can be made to a working paper without the support of the committee.

Yield: During a moderated caucus, a delegate must yield their remaining time. The time can be in one of three ways:

1. to the Chair: the time is disassociated with the delegate and debate continues.

2.   to questions: allows other counties to question the speaker about his/her views.

3.   to another delegate: the speaking time of another country is thereby extended.

What to Wear to a Conference

A Model UN conference is a formal event; not as formal as your sister's wedding, but more formal than a Fourth of July barbeque. Since the way you dress reflects on your character, and the values of your school and the country you represent, it is important that you wear appropriate, professional attire.

Most conferences require delegates to wear western business attire, but some conferences allow delegates to dress in the attire of their country. Whether or not your conference permits national dress, you are required to comply with the standards and dress code of the conference you are to attend. Delegates who do not follow the dress code, or who are dressed improperly, may be asked to leave committee and change into more appropriate attire. In more extreme cases, delegates are excused from the conference and sent home.

Do not put yourself in a situation where you are asked to leave the conference. That is not to say that you should stand at the door of your closet for hours, deliberating what to wear, or stare at your suitcase, obsessing about your wardrobe choices. If you follow this simple guideline, you should be safe: if you would not wear it in front of your grandma, you should not wear it to a Model UN conference. Dress to impress your fellow delegates; you want to make a good first impression. Deciding what to wear to a conference can be the most exciting aspect of preparation, so do not stress about your outfits. Just remember: follow the rules, be professional, and you will not have any problems.

Suggested Attire for Ladies:

- Female suit-set

- Blazer

- Blouse

- Button-up shirt

- Cardigan

- Dress slacks

- Skirt

- Professional dress

You do not need to pack your entire closet to attend a three day conference. Stick to the basics: blazer, pants, blouse, and skirt. Bring a couple choices and mix-and-match! Creating outfits out of a few blouses, pants, and skirts can simplify the packing process, save money, and maximize space in your suitcase.

What not to wear:

- Low-cut dresses or tops

- Crop tops

- T-shirts

- Sweatshirts or sweatpants

- Mini skirts

- Anything see-through

- Jeans

- Shorts

- Sneakers

- Flip-flops

Tips for Ladies:

- Bring a large bag to the conference. You will be surprised by how much you have to carry.

- Bring a bottle of aspirin; especially if you are attending an extended conference (3 or 4 days.) Long committee sessions tend to cause stress headaches.

- Bring a pair of flats to store in your bag, especially if you plan to wear heels. After a day of walking around in five inch heels, your feet will definitely be grateful.

- Bring lots of bandages! Blisters are no fun. If you are wearing heels, you will definitely use them.

- Bring an extra pair of tights or pantyhose. There is nothing worse than having a run in your stocking...

- Bring a cardigan. Committee rooms tend to run on the cooler side, and you do not want to spend the day shivering.

Suggested Attire for Men:

- Suit jacket

- Collared shirt

- Button-down shirt

- Tie

- Slacks

- Dress pants

- Loafers

- Dress shoes

What not to wear:

- T-shirt

- Sweatshirt or sweatpants

- Athletic shorts

- Jeans

- Sneakers

Tips for Men:

- Bring a briefcase. Girls are not the only ones with a lot of stuff to carry! Having a briefcase makes you look businesslike and keeps you organized.

- Wear a suit jacket to committee, even if it is uncomfortable. You look more professional when you wear a suit set, and you can always take the jacket off when you get to the committee room.

- Wear an undershirt. Not only does an undershirt look more polished, it prevents sweat from reaching your expensive button-down shirt.

- Bring a variety of ties. You can always reuse a shirt by pairing it with a new tie.

- Bring an extra pair of socks. Men's dress shoes can be uncomfortable, too! Even if you do not use them, it is always good to have the option.

- Bring shoe polish. Shiny shoes reflect good character.

What to Bring to a Conference

This must be the most consequential question on your mind: what do I need to bring. Although each conference has different rules regarding supplies, there are a few items each delegate should have on hand at a committee session.

Make sure you have:

- your name tag. Some conferences do not let you in the committee room without it.

- your placard. Some conferences prohibit you from voting without it.

- your conference handbook. Keeps you on schedule, and provides valuable information you will need to participate in the conference.

- your research binder. This handy little folder contains all the information you need to debate an issue, and keeps all your research materials in one convenient location. Frequently included materials: country fact sheet, completed country question sheet (page_), topic area summary, and previously proposed solutions.

- your position paper. You should bring at least three copies with you. The best storage location is your research binder.

- blank paper. This is one of the most important supplies you can bring to a conference. Blank paper functions as the canvas on which you write your resolution, or masterpiece, whichever you prefer. Additionally, you will want blank paper to pass notes as it is one of the main channels by which delegates communicate.

- pens and other writing utensils. Crucial tools for a legible resolution.

- a USB drive. Helpful for saving and sharing working papers, draft resolutions, and resolutions.

- a computer (if your conference allows them.)

- a watch. Some conference rooms do not have clocks, which can be irritating for those of us who prefer to know the time.

- a bottle of water. While most conferences do not allow food in the committee room, water is usually permitted.

Additional items you might wish to include on your packing list:

- personalized stationery. Some delegates prefer to have their paper monogramed or stamped with their country's flag. While this tends to be a cosmetic preference, it can save time when passing notes to countries during a committee session.

- index cards. These are also useful for passing notes.

- statistics. It is never a bad idea to bring research with you to a conference. Not only does it help back-up your ideas, it makes you seem engaged and interested in the topic area.

- quotes. Citing a relevant quote can be useful when delivering a speech.

- prepared opening speech. Constructing your address prior to the conference can relieve stress during your first committee session.

- news articles. Can prove to be useful references when speaking to other countries, or at any point during the course of the committee session.

- past resolutions. Critical when crafting a resolution, or corroborating your ideas.

- United Nations Charter. A helpful reference and pleasant reminder of the goals and values of the organization your conference hopes to emulate.

- rules of procedure. It is a great idea to bring a packet about parliamentary procedure. This will prove a valuable tool, especially for novice delegates.

While there will certainly be other supplies you may wish to bring, and I encourage you to include such items on your packing list, these tools serve as a packing guide. Hopefully, this list successfully highlighted the basic necessities you will need at a conference, and directed you to a variety of unique pieces you desire to include in your bag.

What Happens in Each Committee Session?

The chair will have received your position papers beforehand.

The committee will be opened by the Chair.

The Chair and members of the dais will be introduced.

The Chair will take roll of the countries present (roll call.)

The Chair will ask for a motion to set the agenda.

- You may motion to set the agenda by raising your placard and saying: "motion to set the agenda to 'topic area A.'"

- There will be two speakers for and two speakers against the implementation of whichever topic area is proposed.

- After the pro/con debate, you will vote on the topic of debate (Topic area A or B.)

Once the topic area is decided, the chair will open the speaker's list.

- Raise your placard if you would like to be placed on the speaker's list.

After the speaker's list has been exhausted, the chair will then ask for a motion to move into formal debate.

- You can then motion to move into formal debate by raising your placard and saying, "motion to move into formal debate."

Formal Debate:

Once your committee is in formal debate, the chair will then ask a delegate to motion for a moderated caucus.

- You may then motion for a moderated caucus by raising your placard and saying, "Motion for a ten minute moderated caucus on specific topic, speaking time 1 minute.

- The total time, topic, and speaker's time will be different for each moderated caucus.

- Just remember that when you propose a moderated caucus, you need a total time limit, specific topic to discuss, and a specific speaker time.

Once the moderated caucus expires, the chair will ask "if there are any motions on the floor."

- You may then motion for another moderated caucus by raising your placard.

- Make sure that you have a topic, time, and speaking time.

  ○ Try not to motion for consecutive moderated caucuses, give your fellow delegates a chance to motion.

- The chair will most likely entertain a few more moderated caucuses.

After the committee has heard the positions of a variety of countries, the Chair will entertain a motion for an unmoderated caucus.

- The Chair will remind delegates that the purpose of an unmoderated caucus is to speak to other countries or blocs of countries about collaborating on a working paper and eventually a resolution.

- You may motion for an unmoderated caucus by saying, "motion for a 15 minute unmoderated caucus.

- Remember that you need to have a time limit when you motion for an unmoderated caucus.

- Use the time given in an unmoderated caucus to form country blocs and begin drafting a resolution.

In a longer committee session, the chair will start accepting resolutions.

- Committee will proceed as usual after resolutions are accepted, however, debate tends to focus more on specific resolutions than the topic area after country blocs have submitted resolutions.

- It is both acceptable and expected that delegates will motion for both moderated and unmoderated cauci after resolutions are submitted.

In a longer committee session, after resolutions are submitted, the Dais will distribute resolutions to the delegates.

- This gives delegates the opportunity to read the resolutions and educate themselves on the purpose and goals of each respective resolution.

In a longer committee session, the committee will begin voting on resolutions.

- When voting, you vote on amendments first.

  ○ This gives delegates the opportunity to add both friendly and unfriendly amendments to the resolution in question.

- After you vote on the amendments you will vote on the resolution as a whole.

Once voting is completed for a resolution, and the resoultion either passess or fails, the committee will move to vote on each subsequent resolution until all resolutions have been voted on or the designated time for committee has been exhausted.

The chair will then ask if there are any motions on the floor.

- You may then motion for the adjournment of the meeting by saying, "motion for adjournment of the meeting."

This will end the conference.

How to Register for a Conference

Fortunately, anyone can register for a Model UN conference. There are no requirements or necessary prerequisites for a student, class, club, or school to enroll, which means any individual or organization is eligible to join.

Once you have created a team, or decided to participate as a single delegate, you are ready to register for a conference. While the registration process may seem daunting at first glance, it is relatively simple.

First, you need to decide which conference you wish to attend. More than likely, this will be the most difficult step, since choosing a single conference out of the hundreds of symposia is no mean feat.

The best advice I have for finding a Model UN conference is to do your research. No one knows what you are looking for in a conference better than you do, so take the time to learn about the conferences that interest you. Additionally, if you are new to Model UN, I suggest you select a 1 or 2 day conference, instead of a more intense, 4 day conference.

Choosing a shorter, smaller conference will not be as overwhelming as a long, large conference, and will ultimately provide you with the most positive first encounter with Model UN.

One of the easiest ways to learn about conferences is to type "model un conference" into the search engine of your choice. After you enter this phrase, an abundance of choices will be presented. However, if you are struggling to wade through the millions of results that pop-up, there are a few tried-and-true resources you can exploit.

- Best Delegate offers an exhaustive list of conferences organized by date and location. It would be a challenge not to find a relevant conference from their list. http://bestdelegate.com/model-un-conferences-database/
- The United Nations Association of the United States of America also provides delegates with a conference calendar. http://www.unausa.org/global-classrooms-model-un/model-un-conferences/model-un-conference-calendar

After you find the conference that is right for you, or your group, you will need to register for the conference. Some conferences only require your name, address, and contact information in order to register, while other conferences have more extensive applications. No matter the length of the registration, make sure you complete every section of the application, and that the information you enter is accurate.

Once you complete the required form, you will be registered for a conference. Congratulations, after you are enrolled, your delegation will be assigned a country to represent, committee appointment, and topic area summary. The next step in the process is to begin researching your country, topic, and possible solutions.

Here is a breakdown of the registration process:

      1)   Research Model UN conferences.

      2)   Find a conference you want to attend.

      3)   Sign-up for a conference.

      4)   Enter the required information about yourself or your school.

      5)   Submit the application.

      6)   Congratulations! You are now registered for a conference.

Just as anyone can participate in a model un conference, any school, university, non-profit organization has the ability to host a conference.

Where to Start?

Once registered for a Model UN conference, you will most likely be asking yourself this question: What do I do now? Have no fear! While preparing for a conference can seem like a daunting task, there really is no reason to be apprehensive. Even if you have never written a paper, or delivered a speech in front of a committee, you already have most of the skills you will need to participate in a conference. And, I am here to instruct you on the other abilities you will need to effectively conduct yourself in a committee session, and lead you on your journey to your first conference. So buckle-up, because in this chapter we will outline both the requirements and necessary action steps that will prepare you for your conference.

The first step is to begin your research. Fortunately, most conferences distribute background guides to delegates upon registration. If you receive such a packet, that would be a great place to begin your review. If you do not receive a background guide, however, do not fret. While the information included in said folder serves as a wonderful overview and a good place to begin the research process, it by no means covers the depth and breadth of a subject. So, regardless of whether you are presented with a background guide, you will need to conduct a more thorough investigation of your committee, topic area, and country if you desire to be prepared for your conference.

You should begin the research process by learning about the your committee as a whole. Make sure you are familiar with its purpose, programs, and publications. When you have a grasp on the goals and structure of your committee, begin to educate yourself on the topic area you have been assigned. Make sure you have a comprehensive understanding of the issue, and are knowledgeable about past and pending resolutions regarding the topic. The final step of the research process is to learn about your country. Although this is the last piece of the research puzzle, it is the most important. You will need to understand the culture, beliefs, and position of your country in order to accurately act in their interest, and vote in accordance with their values. Remember that at a conference, you are a delegate from another country, and you are required to relinquish your personal views, and assume the role of an ambassador. When you have a firm grasp on your committee, topic area, and country, you will be finished with research. While we will go into more detail about research and the process for researching in the next few chapters, here are some basic things to search for:

- What are the goals of your committee, both as an individual entity, and in terms of the Millennium Development Goals?

- What is your committee's mission statement. What is the purpose of your committee? What does your committee believe?

- What are the past actions of your committee? What has your committee accomplished in the past?

- What are your committee's current efforts? What is your committee focused on today?

- What is the topic area? What is it focused on solving?

- How many people does this issue affect? Is it the global community or a regional section of the population?

- What has been done to address this topic area in the past?

- How do your country's views align with the issue?

- Is your country directly affected by this problem?

- How has your country's government responded to this issue?

- How have your people responded to this topic area?

In conjunction to your research, it is highly recommended that you create a research binder before entering your first committee session. A research binder serves as an organized folio of the facts, maps, statistics, and quotes you found during the research process. Such a folder is a wonderful tool to have at a conference, and serves as a quick reference during debate. Assembling a research binder might seem like a an unnecessary nuisance, but it will be worth your time in the end; and it is actually quite simple to arrange. First, find a binder; three-ringed is preferable. Next, print off valuable information: previous resolutions, your country's profile, inspiring quotes to use when presenting your resolution that will garner support, anything that you will need to present, reference, or possibly use at a conference. Even if this step seems like a hassle now, you will be grateful you put in the extra work; persevere now and reap the rewards at the conference. You never know, a statistic you reference or a quote you make could sway one country's vote, and result in the success of your resolution.

Once you have completed and compiled your research you will be prepared to write a position paper. In essence, a position paper functions as a comprehensive summary of your research. A position paper is divided into three parts: historical background, country's position on a topic, and possible solutions to the problem. Since this document outlines your researching and understanding, it proves extremely useful at a conference, and is a valuable asset during a committee session. Subsequently, because a position paper accurately illustrates your knowledge of the assigned subject, it is often evaluated by the Dias at your conference. So, stick a few extra copies in your research binder, because you never know when you could be evaluated.

The next step in preparing for a conference is writing your opening speech. As the name delineates, your opening speech is your first address to the committee. Each speech typically lasts one minute, and gives you the opportunity to explain your position, country policy, and proposed solution, in regards to the issue, to the delegates in your committee. Ultimately, the opening speech functions as a "first look" at the views of a country, and helps delegates determine who they want to work with on a resolution. While some delegates prefer to draft a unique document, independent of their position paper to emphasize points that would not be addressed otherwise, many delegates use their position paper as their opening speech. Whether you wish to create a new treatise, or utilize your position paper, it is important that you present your views and ideas in a comprehensible manner and highlight points relevant to the resolution you wish to compose. After all, this speech functions as your introduction to the committee members, and connects you with like-minded delegates.

The last thing you will need to learn before a conference is parliamentary procedure. Most likely, this will prove the most challenging step of the process. Since describing parliamentary procedure is complex, and the list of definitions is lengthy, we will not go into detail on this subject until later in the book. However, while we will not address the topic now, keep it in mind as you prepare and read this book; it will come back to haunt you in no time.

These are all the steps you need to take and skills you need to master before walking through the doors to your first committee session. While there are more topics to cover and talents to master for you to participate in a conference, you are now versed on the prerequisites, and are therefore a step closer to participating in your first Model UN conference. Fortunately, we are by no means finished learning about Model UN. Keep your research binder ready, because there are more facts to jot down and information to digest.

Research

After you register for a conference and receive both your country and committee assignments, you will be ready to commence the research process. Researching for a conference may seem like a challenging, time-consuming task, but it is actually one of the most interesting, engaging aspects of the Model UN process; not to mention that it is the most important part of preparation.

It is your duty to research this topic area and familiarize yourself with the issue. This is extremely important, especially if you wish to be a productive member of your committee. Throughout the research process, keep track of the websites, books, or magazines you utilize for quick reference later. If an article, statistic, or quote could be important in your position paper or in the resolution you hope to write, print or copy the facts and store the information in your research binder. Periodically recording and organizing data will save time when you are drafting your resolution or during debate when you are in committee.

When you are researching and preparing for the conference you are to attend, you should focus on three areas:

1)   Your committee as an entity, and its past accomplishments.

2)   Your topic area, including its past, present, and future resolutions.

3)   Your country, its stance on the issue and its role in your assigned committee.

Understanding the committee you are assigned to is a critical aspect of the research process, especially if you want to create a relevant and applicable resolution. Before you arrive at the Model UN conference, make sure you are well versed on your committee's history, function within the United Nations, jurisdiction, goals, and voting procedure. Reading the resolutions your committee has previously enacted can enlighten your understanding of your committee's powers, typical actions, and the methods by which it acts.

The topic area you are assigned was selected to expose you to an important issue or wide-reaching problem that faces the global community. More than likely, the first place you will learn about your topic area is in the background guide you are given when you register for a conference. Although this is a great way to begin your research, you will need to augment your understanding of the issue with a variety of additional resources, including books, magazines, and online articles. During the research process, ask yourself these questions to make sure you are gathering enough information.

●   What solutions have already been proposed to address this topic area?

●   How does this problem affect my country?

- What has my country done to address this issue?

Once you understand the past efforts of your committee and the scope of your topic area, you will be ready to delve into your country's views on the issue. This is a crucial step in the research process because a delegate must understand the policies of their country in order to accurately represent their beliefs. During this process, you will want to learn about your country's allies, culture, economy, history, and policies. Ask yourself these questions throughout the exercise to ensure you are gathering pertinent information.

- Is my country directly affected by this issue?

- How has my country dealt with this issue in the past/How does my country currently deal with this issue?

- How has my country tried to resolve this issue in the past?

- How can my country help other countries that are affected by this issue?

- Has a United Nations representative from my country already addressed this issue?

- Has my country supported past United Nations resolutions regarding this topic?

- How have my country's allies responded to this issue?

The most difficult part of your research, however, will be determining your country's implicit position on the topic area you are to debate. A country's position on an issue is often implicit, or not explicitly stated in any document, for a variety of reasons. No matter the reason why your country does not have a concrete stance on an issue, it behoves you to determine the most probable position your country would take based on its culture, economic interests, history, and political views.

By this point, after absorbing leagues of information regarding your committee, topic area, and country, you should have an idea of the position you will take during your conference. The next step in conference preparation is writing a position paper, but before you tackle that behemoth, take a moment to review your notes and data. This final step will ensure you have an adequate understanding of your position.

Evaluating your work is actually quite simple, all you have to do is confirm you have answered the "Five Crucial W's":

- Who? Which countries, ethnic groups, non-governmental organizations, and people will be affected by this issue?

- What? What is this issue about? What started the conflict? What has been done to resolve the problem?

- When? When did this problem begin? When will it become critical, if it is not already?

- Where? Where did this issue originate? Is the conflict confined to one geographical area, or is it a global problem?

- Why? Why is this issue significant? Why should the United Nations focus their time and energy on addressing and solving this problem?

Once you have reviewed your research, and substantiated the position you will take at the conference, you will be prepared to summarize your findings in one comprehensive document, affectionately titled: the position paper.

Helpful Questions to Jumpstart Your Research

Fill out these questions about your country, topic, and solutions before a conference in order to guide your research and augment your position paper.

1. What is your country's official name?

2. What is the size of your country? (in square miles)

3. What is the location of your country?

   a. If your country is small or its location is not common knowledge, it might be helpful to print off a map to show other delegates.

4. Who are your country's neighbors?

5. What is the population of your country?

6. What is the official language of your country?

7. What is your country's capital?

8. When was your country founded?

9. What type of government does your country have?

10. Who is/are your country's leader(s)?

11.   Who are your country's allies/enemies?

12.   What is your country's currency?

13.   What are your country's natural resources?

14.   What is the climate of your country?

15.   What is the highest/lowest elevation of your country?

16.   What is the average life expectancy in your country?

17.   What is/are the gross domestic product(s) of your country?

18.   What are your country's imports/exports?

19.   What is your country's position on your topic area

       a.   an example topic area would be Nuclear Proliferation or the Spread of Infectious Diseases

20.   How has your country dealt with the topic area in the past?

21.   What actions has your country taken to address your topic area?

22.   What solutions to your topic area does your country support?

23.   What solutions to your topic area does your country oppose?

24.   How does your country hope to resolve this issue?

Example of a Completed Country Question Sheet

Country: United Kingdom

Committee: General Assembly

Topic: Nuclear Proliferation

1.   What is your country's official name?

The United Kingdom of Great Britain and Northern Ireland.

2.   What is the size of your country? (in square kilometers)

The total area is 243,610 square kilometers. The United Kingdom is twice the size of Pennsylvania.

3.   What is the location of your country?

The United Kingdom is an island in the Northeast Atlantic Ocean. It shares a border with Ireland, and is separated from France by the English Channel.

4.   Who are your country's neighbors?

Ireland, France, Belgium, Netherlands, and Germany.

5.   What is the population of your country?

As of July 2014, the estimated population is 63,742,977.

6.   What is the official language of your country?

English.

7.   What is your country's capital?

London.

8.   When was your country founded?

On March 3, 1284, England and Wales were united with the enactment of the Statute of

Rhuddlan. In 1536, the Act of Union formally incorporated England and Wales. On May

1, 1707 England and Scotland are united as Great Britain by the Acts of Union. On

January 1, 1801, Great Britain and Ireland are united and become the United Kingdom

of Great Britain and Ireland. On December 6, 1921 the Anglo-Irish Treaty formalizes

partition of Ireland. On April 12, 1927 the Royal and Parliamentary Titles Act

established the current name of the United Kingdom of Great Britain and Northern

Ireland.

9.   What type of government does your country have?

Constitutional monarchy, and Commonwealth realm.

10.   Who is/are your country's leader(s)?

David Cameron, Prime Minister.

11.   Who are your country's allies/enemies?

Allies: United States, Israel, France, Canada

Enemies: Iran, Russia, North Korea

12.   What is your country's currency?

Pound sterling.

13.   What are your country's natural resources?

The United Kingdom's natural resources are: coal, petroleum, natural gas, iron ore, lead, zinc, gold, tin, limestone, salt, clay, chalk, gypsum, potash, silica sand, slate, arable land.

14.   What is the climate of your country?

Overall, the climate is temperate; moderated by prevailing southwest winds over the North Atlantic Current. More than one-half of the days are overcast.

15.   What is the highest/lowest elevation of your country?

Highest point: Ben Nevis 1,343 m.

Lowest point: The Fens -4 m.

16.   What is the average life expectancy in your country?

The life expectancy at birth for the total population is 80.42 years.

17.   What is/are the gross domestic product(s) of your country?

Cereals, oilseed, poultry, fish, potatoes, vegetables, cattle, sheep, machine tools, electric power equipment, automation equipment, railroad equipment, shipbuilding, aircraft, motor vehicles and parts, electronics and communications equipment, metals, chemicals, coal, petroleum, paper and paper products, food processing, textiles, clothing.

18.   What are your country's imports/exports?

Imports: manufactured goods, machinery, fuels; foodstuffs.

Exports: manufactured goods, fuels, chemicals; food, beverages, tobacco.

19.   What is your country's position on Nuclear Proliferation?

The United Kingdom wants to stop the spread of chemical, biological, radiological and nuclear (CBRN) weapons and ballistic missiles. The United Kingdom believes that the spread of such weapons creates serious humanitarian and security concerns.

20.   How has your country dealt with Nuclear Proliferation in the past?

The United Kingdom is involved in the Global Partnership, a multilateral non-proliferation initiative created in June 2002. This organization funds projects to prevent terrorists and other proliferators from acquiring (CBRN) weapons and materials of mass destruction. Additionally, the government published its National Counter-Proliferation Strategy in March 2012. The goals of this strategy are: to deny terrorists the materials to make WMD; to stop countries from obtaining WMD or other advanced conventional weapons; and to help to protect global security and prosperity.

21.   What actions has your country taken to address Nuclear Proliferation?

The United Kingdom is involved in the Nuclear Non-Proliferation Treaty. The United Kingdom has crafted and contributed to a number of documents that address the problem of nuclear proliferation.

22.   What solutions to Nuclear Proliferation does your country support?

The United Kingdom supports the solution that will eradicate all nuclear weapons. Ultimately, the United Kingdom hopes to stop the spread and development of all CBRN in unapproved nations.

23.   What solutions to Nuclear Proliferation does your country oppose?

The United Kingdom asserts that the only solution to the problem of nuclear proliferation is to confiscate weapons from unapproved countries, stop the development of CBRN, and consolidate all weapons to countries that are equipped to handle the responsibility.

24.   How does your country hope to resolve Nuclear Proliferation?

The United Kingdom hopes to take inventory of all nuclear weapons and weapons of mass destruction, confiscate weapons from countries that are unprepared to handle and store such weapons, and eliminate any further development of nuclear weapons, or any other weapons of mass destruction.

Helpful Online Resources

Websites:

https://www.cia.gov/library/publications/the-world-factbook/

http://www.un.org/Depts/dhl/

http://research.un.org/en

http://www.library.northwestern.edu/libraries-collections/evanston-campus/government-information/international-documents

http://www.worldbank.org/en/research

http://www.state.gov/r/pa/ei/bgn/

http://news.bbc.co.uk/2/hi/country_profiles/

https://www.oxfam.org/

http://www.unfoundation.org/

http://www.unausa.org/

http://www.cfr.org/publication/

http://www.un.org/News/

http://bestdelegate.com/research/

http://www.un.org/en/hq/dpi/

http://www.un.int/

http://www.unausa.org/images/content/GC_Model_UN/Resources/Permanent_Missions.pdf

What is a Position Paper?

A position paper, sometimes called a point of view paper, is a one-to-two page summary of your country's history and current position on the topic you are to debate in committee. Ultimately, a position paper is a cohesive document containing information about your country, your country's position on the topic area, and solutions your country supports. Crafting a position paper is not only a wonderful way to compile information, but will prove an invaluable tool at the conference you are to attend.

Upon completing your research, you should begin composing a position paper. Your position paper should be organized into three parts: background of your topic, measures taken by your country to address your topic, and how you plan to resolve the topic during committee.

A position paper is an incredibly helpful document. It will not only refresh your memory on the extensive research you did on your country, but it will inform the other delegates in your committee about your country's position on the topic area. Sharing your position paper with a delegate will help jump-start a conversation, and reading your position paper to the committee as an entity will help you facilitate a committee-wide discussion.

How to Write a Position Paper

While writing a position paper may seem like a daunting task at first glance, it is actually quite simple. All you have to do is research your country, compile the information you find, and type your recommendations into a brief, comprehensive document.

Don't believe that you are capable of constructing an article of this nature? Well, by the end of this chapter, you will not only be capable of such a feat, but you will be able to instruct your friends, family, and neighbors on the proper way to produce a position paper.

First things first, format. Position papers must follow a specific format, which makes them both easy to produce and understand. The format in-itself is quite simple, consisting of the header and the body of the paper.

Format of a Position Paper:

<u>Header:</u> In the top left hand corner of the page write the name(s) of your delegation, country, committee, date, and topic.

<u>The body of the paper.</u>

I. **The Historical Background:** In this paragraph elaborate on the background of the topic from the position of your country. Answer questions like: How has my country been involved with this issue? What is my country's history with this topic?

II. **Country's Position on the Topic:** In this paragraph explain how your nation is currently being effected by the topic area. Answer questions like: How has this issue affected my country? What is my country's stance on the topic? What steps has my country already taken to address, or overcome this issue? What have been the benefits of these actions? How could these actions be extended or improved?

III. **Possible Solutions to the Topic:** In the final paragraph of your position paper, you should propose a variety of solutions you believe the United Nations should consider. You should also include how your country will collaborate with other countries on this issue. Answer questions like: What actions do I want the United Nations to take in order to resolve this issue? What solutions do my country support? What solutions would my country oppose? How will I work implement these strategies? How will I collaborate with other countries?

    A.   These goals do not necessarily need to be realistic. However, they should be goals that your nation is willing to pursue.

Next, review your research. How can you take your new knowledge, and shape it into the established format of a position paper? Begin by outlining your findings. Even skilled MUNers struggle to form their research and ideas into a properly formatted paper. By creating an outline of your paper before you start writing, and avoid any possible digressions, and let's be honest, you don't have the time or the space to ramble in this paper. Once you have created a road map to follow, you are well on your way to writing a winning position paper.

Finally, begin writing. Put pen to paper, or fingers to keys. The hardest part of creating a position paper is getting started. Avoid writer's block by jotting down notes and facts about your country to rev-up your brain. Do not be discouraged if it takes you a couple days to complete your position paper. This is a challenging task, and you should not be finished within thirty minutes of starting. If you ever find yourself staring at your sheet of paper, or computer screen, get up and move on to a different task. You have plenty of time to complete and revise your position paper. There is no way you procrastinated until the night before it is due, right?

If you do find yourself scrambling to finish your paper. Don't have a panic attack. This is not the final ten-page research paper in your AP English class. This is a short, comprehensive overview of your country's position on a topic. Your position paper is meant to benefit you. So, do not worry about having a perfect paper, even if it is being graded. Ultimately, the graders review your paper to ascertain whether you prepared for the conference or not. They will not be cross-checking your facts, or determining whether or not your used an Oxford comma correctly. That is not to say that your facts should be inaccurate, or that you should not use proper grammar, but do not obsess about the minute details of your paper. After all, it is more for your benefit than it is for the reviewer, and most importantly, it is not for a grade.

Helpful Tips:

- Complete the research on your country and topic before you begin writing your position paper.

- Outline your position paper before writing it.

  ○ This will help solidify your facts and ideas which will help your create a more cohesive position paper.

- Ensure that your position paper reflects the views of your country NOT your personal views.

- Refrain from using first person pronouns.

- Try to propose creative solutions. The committee session will be more engaging if you suggest resolutions that have not implemented by the United Nations or previously debated.

- Aim to craft a concise paper, so you do not bore your reader or fellow delegates, but make sure you thoroughly outline your position and solutions. Feel free to use dates, names, or titles if you believe they are necessary.

- Begin writing your position paper early. Most conferences require position papers to be submitted prior to the conference, so the Secretariat will have time to review and grade each proposal.

Review of a Position Paper Outline

I. History

A.   This paragraph summarizes how your country has dealt with the topic in the past.

II. Present Situation

A.   In this paragraph, you detail the current condition of your country in regards to the topic.

III. Proposed Solution

A.   The concluding paragraph should outline possible resolutions while addressing conceivable obstacles that your country, or the global community, will face while amending the issue.

Example Position Papers

Example Position Paper #1:

Name: Vivian Armitage

Country: Syria

Committee: World Health Organization

Date: January 9, 2014

Topic Area: Topic Area A: Illegal Organ Trade

Syria has been gripped by Civil War since the Arab Spring uprisings began in March 2011. Syria has a population of almost 23 million people, two-thirds of whom are Sunni Muslim. The sectarian nature of the Syrian civil war violence has contributed to increased Shiite/Sunni tensions throughout the Middle East. The UN fears that the Syrian conflict could easily flow into Lebanon, Iraq, Turkey, and Jordan. Many believe the roots of the conflict reach back to the beginning of the 20th century. It wasn't until 1946 that Syria obtained independence from French colonial rule. Between 1946 and 1958, Syria suffered several military coups before it briefly formed a union with Egypt. In September 1961, Egypt and Syria separated, and the Syrian Arab Republic was created. Syria has been in conflict with Israel since the creation of the Jewish state in 1948. As a result of the 1967 Arab-Israeli War, Syria lost the Golan Heights to Israel. Since 1964 an UN Disengagement Observer Force has patrolled a buffer zone between the two countries. In July 2000, following the death of President al-Assad, his son, Bashar al-Assad, was approved as president by popular referendum, with a special exception made for his age. Bashar al-Assad was elected to a second term in May 2007. Since late 2011, the Arab League, EU, Turkey, and the United States have levied economic sanctions against the Assad regime. Syria has been a close ally of Iran and Russia for decades adding to tensions between world powers. Syria has hundreds of armed rebel groups without a unified commander. The Syrian Civil War has continued throughout 2013. The death toll among Syrian Government forces, opposition forces, and civilians has topped 100,000.

Syria has a myriad of problems with which to contend. Syria has fewer than 1.5 health workers per 1,000 inhabitants. The World Health Organization estimates that fewer than 2.3 health workers (physicians, nurses, and midwives only) per 1,000 is insufficient to achieve coverage of primary health care needs. There has been an international awareness about the problems that stem from selling human body parts for decades. The WHO issued guidelines in 1991 to avoid the exploitation of organ donors. 192 countries signed the document; however the guidelines are not binding and the recommendations have been ignored. There is no international document that addressed international organ transplantation. In 2003 the UN Protocol to Prevent, Suppress, and Punish Trafficking in Persons also addressed the issue. 117 countries signed it. In 2008, as an extension of the WHO 2004 resolution, the International Society of Nephrology and Transplantation Society hosted a Summit in Istanbul to address the global problem of organ trafficking. The resulting Declaration on Organ Trafficking and Transplant Tourism prohibited "organ trafficking because the act exploits the poor and vulnerable, and therefore violates the principles of equity and justice for human dignity. Signed by only 92 organizations it is not legally binding. The situation in Syria is similar to what happened to Somali refugees in Egypt. Where there is poverty and ignorance there is exploitation.

The lucrative nature of organ transplantation and the fact that it is illegal has attracted a criminal element. According to the University of California Berkeley there are several well established international rings that specialize in transplant tourism. Israeli patients travel to Turkey where they purchase Russian kidneys; Israelis also travel to NY to receive illegally harvested organs. EU and American patients go to the Philippines where poor locals sell their organs. Wealthy Arabs travel to Iraq to purchase organs from refugees. There is also a thriving black market in India. Legalizing the sale of human organs would cause it to be regulated. Iran has a legal system of buying and selling human body parts. Another solution would be to reduce the demand for transplantation. Education of diet and physical activity could be a solution. Education about the risks and dangers involved in organ selling is another potential solution. There also should be a way to punish medical professionals involved in illegal organ transplants. In 2013 Canada prosecuted several human organ traffickers in Kosovo. This case resulted in prison time. The patients paid over $150,000 for the kidney whereas the victims received less than $10,000. The UN feels that the "legal pillars of a proposed treaty should be prevention, protections and prosecution."

Example Position Paper #2:

Name: Vivian Armitage

VIVIAN ARMITAGE

Country: Andorra

Committee: World Health Organization

Date: November 24, 2014

Topic Area: Topic Area A: Infectious Diseases

Andorra is a sovereign microstate, landlocked in Southwestern Europe. Andorra is located in the eastern Pyrenees mountains, in-between Spain and France. As Andorra is the sixth smallest nation in Europe, it has not had many infectious disease outbreaks. With this being said, the greatest medical threat in Andorra is food poisoning. According to General Council Law on Communicable Infectious and Transmissible Diseases, foodborne infections and intoxications are listed as mandatorily notified communicable diseases. Some of the communicable diseases that pose a threat include: brucellosis, cholera, bacilar and amoebic dysentery. There was an instance between 2001 and 2009 when Andorra felt threatened by a major disease outbreak. This was due to the fact that the Principality of Andorra is surrounded by areas in which Pyrenean chamois populations were severely affected by infection with border disease virus (BDV) which caused many disease outbreaks. Fortunately, Andorra has not had to grapple with widespread disease outbreak.

In most regions of the world, besides South Asia and sub-Saharan Africa, diabetes, cardiovascular disease, and cancer are among a group of chronic diseases that accounts for most deaths. Alternately, infectious diseases and other traditional killers are claiming fewer lives in developed and developing countries where numbers of death from chronic diseases is rising. Additionally, the world's elderly population, who is more prone to chronic disease, continues to grow. For this reason, deadly infectious diseases that rampage undeveloped nations, do not get as much attention as the increasing number of deaths from heart attacks. This is the problem, our world needs to help those who do not have the materials or ability to help themselves; especially the countries that are forced to battle such devastating diseases. Andorra believes that we should provide aid to these struggling nations. Even though, according to the Centers for Disease Control and Prevention, there are no travel warnings or restrictions within the Principality of Andorra. Since Andorra has very little risk for any disease outbreak in its own land, it is willing and prepared to provide aid to countries afflicted with rampaging disease.

Due to the potentially widespread and fatal consequences of a disease outbreak, it is crucial that every nation has a plan to deal with such a situation. If every country were to adopt disease prevention measures, such as posting hygiene signs to inform people of the proper way to wash their hands. As well as creating a team of first responders who would be equipped with the necessary tools if an outbreak should occur, the world would be better prepared to deal with such an event. Provided that there were universal rules and regulations regarding the required response to a disease outbreak, the risk of the spread of infection would decrease and the world population in general would be spared from a potentially catastrophic event.

Example Position Paper #3:

Name: Edward Armitage

Country: Andorra

Committee: Legal Committee

Date: January 29, 2015

Topic Area: Topic Area A: International Terrorism

Andorra is an independent, incredibly small, country. Landlocked, Andorra is located next to France and Spain in the mountainous region of Europe. Andorra has a relatively small population. So small, in fact, that it is often overlooked. Its life expectancy is incredibly high, which makes sense, because it is a small country. And Andorra has a literacy rate of one hundred percent. Andorra has been an independent nation since 1278.

International Terrorism is currently not a huge issue in Andorra, and it really isn't on the top of their 'deal with' or 'to do' lists. International terrorism is usually seen in larger countries because they have more resources. While the two countries surrounding Andorra, France and Spain, may be susceptible to terrorism, it is highly unlikely that Andorra will be affected by such an event. Ultimately, Andorra does not plan to get involved in any of the possible disputes that could arise.

This being said, Andorra proposes an Interagency committee with European countries, such as Andorra, as to being the process of combating this issue. These committees would devote their time to tracking down international terrorist groups and finding further ways to combat the international terrorist threat. Andorra believes that this is the best possible way to regulate any potential threats, hopefully preventing a terrorist attack.

What is Parliamentary Procedure?

Parliamentary procedure serves as the language delegates use to communicate at a Model UN conference. Ultimately, parliamentary procedure is a set of guidelines that regulates debate, facilitates smooth transitions, and ensures equality among committee members. In order to actively participate in a Model UN conference, you must have a working knowledge of the rules of procedure. Along with maintaining standards and promoting decorum in a committee, the rules of procedure were enacted to guarantee that all member states are treated fairly and are awarded an equal chance to voice both their opinions and concerns. Meaning, each member state regardless of size, population, or wealth is recognized in accordance to established mandates.

Delegates are required to learn the language of parliamentary procedure in conjunction with their topic area research and country study. This qualification was established in order to provide students with a comprehensive understanding of the workings of the United Nations, on both an investigative and administrative level.

Although it will take practice and a few iterations of review to feel comfortable with the material, once you grasp the process, parliamentary procedure will become second nature to you. While it may seem like a daunting, insurmountable task now, if you stick with it and review often, you will be a parliamentary procedure pro in no time. Now, before you are introduced to a catalogue of definitions, and we begin memorizing a procedural lexicon, let us introduce you to the 10 governing rules of parliamentary procedure:

1.   The interests of the committee as a whole supercede those of an individual delegate.

2.   All member states have equal obligations, privileges, and rights.

3.   Only one member state may be recognized to speak at a time.

4.   The committee may only recognize one motion at a time.

5.   When committee is in session, personal proposals, remarks, or retorts are out of order.

6.   Each debatable motion must be debated.

7.   Abstention equates to acceptance.

8.   After a vote has been passed/failed it may not be further debated in the committee.

9.   The Minority maintain the right to debate and oppose any issue.

10.   Ultimately, however, the Majority rules.

Keep these rules in mind as we wade through a breadth of knowledge. Additionally, remember this quote, delivered by Henry M. Robert, himself, on the goals of these governing laws of decorum.

"American Parliamentary Law is built upon the principle that rights must be respected: rights of the majority, of the minority, of individuals, of absentees, and rights of all these together." ~Henry M. Robert, Rules of Order Revised (1951.)

These regulations will serve you well throughout your whole life. Not only will they allow you to properly participate in a conference, but they will show you the importance of tolerance, fairness, and impartiality when conducting a meeting. Thereby providing you with the fundamental knowledge necessary to succeed in the global marketplace. Now, let us dive into the glorious tenets of parliamentary procedure.

Parliamentary Procedure in Translation

Standard Point: I need to use the bathroom.

Using Parliamentary Procedure: Point of Personal Privilege, may I use the bathroom?

Standard Point: You cannot hear the Chinese delegation

Using Parliamentary Procedure: Point of Personal Privilege, the delegates in the back of the room cannot hear the Chinese delegation.

Standard Point: The room is too hot.

Using Parliamentary Procedure: Point of Personal Privilege, can we turn the air conditioning on? The room is a bit hot.

Standard Point: You wish to set the agenda.

Using Parliamentary Procedure: Honorable Chair, the delegate of (your country's name) moves to set the agenda.

Standard Point: You wish to open the Speaker's List.

Using Parliamentary Procedure: Honorable Chair, the delegate of (your country's name) moves to open the Speaker's List and begin debate.

Standard Point: You wish to close the Speaker's List.

Using Parliamentary Procedure: Honorable Chair, the delegate of (your country's name) moves to close the Speaker's List move into formal debate.

Standard Point: The delegate of China rose on the wrong point.

Using Parliamentary Procedure: Point of Order, the delegate of China rose on the wrong point, can he/she please clarify what he/she meant.

Standard Point: The Dais uses the wrong term when explaining the topic of the moderated caucus.

Using Parliamentary Procedure: Honorable Chair, the delegate from (your country's name) has a Point of Order, could you please explain what the topic of our moderated caucus?I think you stated the wrong topic.

Standard Point: The delegate of Indonesia is being inappropriate.

Using Parliamentary Procedure: Point of Order, the delegate of Indonesia has used inappropriate language.

Standard Point: The delegate of France was verbally abused by the delegate of Argentina.

Using Parliamentary Procedure: Right of Reply, the delegate of Argentina has offended the delegate of France.

Standard Point: The delegate of Canada offends your delegation.

Using Parliamentary Procedure: Right of Reply, the delegate of Canada has offended my delegation by using inappropriate language.

Standard Point: You wish to introduce a working paper, amendment or resolution to the committee.

Using Parliamentary Procedure: Honorable Chair, the delegate of (your country's name) moves to introduce working paper/amendment/resolution to the committee.

Standard Point: You wish to end debate on a topic.

Using Parliamentary Procedure: Honorable Chair, (your country's name) moves to table the topic of (topic) and discuss it at a later time.

Standard Point: You have a question for a delegate who just concluded his/her speech.

Using Parliamentary Procedure: Honorable Chair, (your country name) has a point of information for the delegate from (their country's name.)

Standard Point: You don't know what is going on in committee.

Using Parliamentary Procedure: Point of Parliamentary Inquiry, what is the next event on the agenda?

Standard Point: You have a question regarding the rules of procedure.

Using Parliamentary Procedure: Honorable Chair, the delegate from (your country's name) has a Point of Inquiry.

Standard Point: You wish to close debate and move into voting procedure.

Using Parliamentary Procedure: Honorable Chair, (your country name) moves to Close Debate and move into Voting Procedure.

Standard Point: You want to end the final committee session of the whole conference (do NOT use this unless it is the end of the LAST session.)

Using Parliamentary Procedure: Motion for Adjournment of Meeting.

Standard Point: You want to end the committee session (do NOT use this unless it is the end of the committee session.)

Using Parliamentary Procedure: Motion for Suspension of Meeting.

Standard Point: You want to propose an Unmoderated Caucus.

Using Parliamentary Procedure: Motion for an Unmoderated Caucus, topic: discussion of working paper 1.3; time: 15 minutes.

Standard Point: You want to propose a Moderated Caucus.

Using Parliamentary Procedure: Motion for Moderated Caucus, topic: illegal organ trade in the Middle East; time: 10 minutes; speaking time: 30 seconds.

Standard Point: You wish to yield the time remaining after your speech.

Using Parliamentary Procedure: Honorable Chair, (your country name) yields his/her time to (the Chair/questions/the delegate from (delegate's country name.))

Standard Point: You want to vote on the resolution that is being debated.

Using Parliamentary Procedure: Motion to move into voting procedure on Resolution 2.3.

Standard Point: You want to set the order in which you debate topics in committee.

Using Parliamentary Procedure: Motion to Set the Agenda to topic area A, the illegal organ trade.

Standard Point: You want to make sure the vote was counted accurately.

Using Parliamentary Procedure: The delegate of (your country's name) moves for a roll call vote.

Standard Point: You want to vote on portions of a resolution, rather than voting on the resolution as a whole.

Using Parliamentary Procedure: Honorable Chair, the delegate from (your country's name) moves to divide the question on resolution number (resolution #.)

Standard Point: You want to reintroduce a proposal that has either been accepted or rejected by the committee.

Using Parliamentary Procedure: Honorable Chair, the delegate from (your country's name) moves to reconsider amendment/resolution number (amendment/resolution #.)

Parliamentary Procedure Definitions

Motions:

- **Motion to set the agenda**: Determines which topic your committee will debate first.

    ○ There will be two speakers for and two against the proposed motion.

- **Motion to call for orders of the day**: Compels the committee to return to the agenda when debate has digressed from the approved topic-area.

    ○ A delegate may interrupt a speaker with this motion.

- **Motion to open the speaker's list**: Used when a delegate wants to begin debating the chosen topic.

    ○ Each delegate who wishes to speak about the topic or their country's view on the topic should raise their placard. The chair will add each country who wishes to speak to the speaker's list.

- **Motion to close the speaker's list**: Raised when a delegate does not want any other countries to be added to the speaker's list.

- ○ Once each of the countries on the speaker's list have spoken, the committee will automatically move into voting procedure.

- **Motion to Limit or Extend the Time of Debate**: Used to limit the number of times a delegate is permitted to speak, the number of speakers, the length of a speech, or the length of debate on a resolution or topic.

  - ○ Such a motion requires a ⅔ majority.

  - ○ Additionally, this motion is debatable.

- **Motion to suspend the rules**: Raised when the rules governing the committee prevent the committee from accomplishing necessary business.

  - ○ The rules of the <u>Charter of the United Nations</u> and those regarding voting procedure will remain in effect.

- **Motion to appeal**: Used to challenge a decision made by the Chair, or to correct procedural mistakes made by the Chair.

  - ○ A delegate would be advised to seriously consider the consequences of this motion before he/she makes the proposal.

  - ○ Pointing-out the mistakes of the Chair can be detrimental to the delegate who made the motion and alter the committee dynamics as a whole.

- **Motion to Caucus**: Presented if a delegate wishes to debate a working paper, draft resolution, or resolution.

  - ○ During a caucus, delegates can revise, amend, or combine resolutions.

  - ○ When the committee is in a caucus, delegates are not permitted to leave the room.

- **Motion for a Moderated Caucus**: Proposed when a delegate wishes to discuss a specific aspect of the topic area.

  - You can rise on this motion at any point during the course of debate, or after the Dais asks if there are any points or motions on the floor.

  - You need to provide specifics when proposing a moderated caucus, including the: purpose of the caucus, total length of the caucus, and speaker time.

  - Moderated caucuses are a wonderful medium to generate discussion. Especially if you want to address or debate a specific aspect of the topic area with the entire committee.

- **Motion for Unmoderated Caucus**:

  - You can rise on this motion at any point during the course of debate, or after the Dais asks if there are any points or motions on the floor.

  - You need to provide specifics when proposing an unmoderated caucus, including the: purpose of the caucus, total length of the caucus, and speaker time.

  - Unmoderated caucuses are a great way to initiate a dialogue with your fellow delegates. During an unmoderated caucus, you can begin to formulate working papers and resolutions.

- **Motion to introduce a working paper, amendment, or resolution**: Introduced when a delegate, or block of delegates, wants to debate a working paper, draft resolution, amendment, or resolution with the committee.

- Propose this motion after the Dais has distributed the working papers, draft resolutions, or resolutions.

- Be specific about which document you want to introduce.

  - Example: motion to introduce working paper 3.1

- **Motion to table a topic**: Submitted when a delegate wishes to stop debate on a topic, or wishes to change the topic area.

  - This motion may be proposed at any time during the course of committee.

  - There will be two pro speakers and two con speakers for this motion.

  - If this motion passes, there will be no votes on any of the working papers, draft resolutions, or amendments that the committee had been debating prior to the motion. The present topic will become void and the committee will automatically transition to the new topic area and begin debate.

- **Motion to take from the table**: A delegate may make a motion of this nature if he/she wishes to reintroduce a proposal or draft resolution that was previously tabled by the committee.

  - This motion is only in order if there is no unfinished business on the floor.

  - Additionally, a motion to take from the table requires a majority vote, and is debatable.

- **Motion to postpone debate**: Introduced when a delegate wishes to discuss a topic at a later time.

- A delegate must establish a time when debate on the subject will resume. When that time is reached, debate will resume if the floor is not occupied, and the committee is not in voting procedure.

- A motion of this nature is only applicable to agenda topics and resolutions.

- **Motion to adopt by acclamation**: Used to pass motions without voting.

  - During a motion to adopt by acclamation, the Chair will tap his/her gavel three times and ask the committee if there are any objections.

  - If any member of the committee objects, the motion will fail and the committee will move into voting procedure.

  - This motion may only be proposed when the committee is in voting procedure.

- **Motion to close debate and move into voting procedure**: Proposed when a delegate wants to end debate on a topic, and vote on the proposed resolutions.

  - There will be two pro and con speakers for this motion.

- **Motion for a roll call vote**: Used in place of a placard vote.

  - With a roll call vote, each country's name will be called and delegates will vote individually rather than as an entity. A country may vote in one of five ways: yes, yes with rights, no, no with rights, and pass.

    - A vote of yes/no with rights means that a delegate can defend his/her vote after the votes have been tallied. When the vote has been closed, a delegate who voted with rights may give a thirty second speech substantiating their decision.

- ○ The Chair must move to approve of this motion before it is implemented.

- **Motion to move to previous question**: Allows the committee to move into voting procedure.

  - ○ This motion may only be considered after one pro and one con speaker have debated the proposal.

  - ○ Additionally, this motion requires a second, and a two-thirds majority.

- **Motion to divide the question**: Submitted when a delegate wants to vote on portions of a resolution, rather than voting on the resolution as a whole.

  - ○ A delegate may use this motion if he/she agrees with the majority of a resolution, but disagrees with certain clauses.

  - ○ This motion requires two speakers for and two speakers against the proposal.

- **Motion to reconsider**: Reintroduces a proposal that has either been accepted or rejected by the committee.

  - ○ This motion may only be made by a representative who voted on the prevailing side of the vote.

  - ○ Additionally, such a motion is only applicable when there are not other proposals on the floor.

- **Motion to withdraw a proposal**: May be made by the sponsor of said proposal at any time before the committee moves into voting procedure.

- ○ A motion that has been withdrawn may be reintroduced by any delegate.

- **Motion for Suspension of Meeting**: Used to suspend committee proceedings until the next scheduled session.
  - ○ The Chair must specifically ask for a " motion to suspend the meeting" for this motion to be valid.
  - ○ If this motion is called prematurely, the Dais will rule it out of order.

- **Motion for Adjournment of Meeting**: Raised to conclude the entire Model UN conference until the next year.
  - ○ The chair must specifically ask for a " motion to adjourn the meeting" for this motion to be valid.
  - ○ Do NOT use this motion until the last committee session, or it will be ruled dilatory.

Points:

- **Point of Personal Privilege**: Used to address an issue that prevents a delegate from proceeding with debate.
  - ○ A delegate may rise on this point at any time during committee; even when another delegate is speaking.
  - ○ A possible point of personal privilege could be an inability to hear the speaker, or physical discomfort.
  - ○ Since these points can be distracting, try to use them sparingly.

- **Point of Clarification**: Introduced to clarify an error in a working paper, draft resolution, or an amendment.

- ○ These points are helpful when fixing grammatical or clausal errors.

- ○ This point may only be raised on after a resolution or amendment is introduced, otherwise it is irrelevant.

- **Point of Information**: Proposed when a delegate has a question for a speaker regarding their position or resolution.

- **Follow-up**: Submitted after the speaker has responded to a *Point of Information*.

  - ○ A follow-up is used to further question a speaker, and may only be used immediately following a *Point of Information*.

  - ○ Although a follow-up is not technically a point, it is recognized as such in the order of procedure.

  - ○ A delegate is allowed one follow-up per *Point of Information*.

- **Point of Order**: Enacted when a delegate wishes to address an improper proposal or a violation of parliamentary procedure, whether by a fellow delegate, or by the dais.

  - ○ Since this is a serious point to rise on, do not use this suggestion unless you are certain that the rules of procedure have been violated.

- **Point of Parliamentary Inquiry**: A delegate may rise on this point if he/she has a question regarding the rules of procedure, or needs to clarify a question regarding the matters being discussed by the committee.

  - ○ A delegate may make this point at any time during a committee session.

Yields:

A yield is utilized when a delegate has time remaining after their speech during a moderated caucus. A delegate may yield his/her time one of four ways: to the chair, to questions, to another delegate, or to comments. If a delegate neglects to yield his/her time, the time will be appointed to comments.

- **Yield to the chair**: The chair will receive the remaining speaking time. Essentially, the time is nullified and there is no further discussion on a delegate's speech.

- **Yield to questions**: Allows other delegates to use the extra time to ask the speaker questions regarding his/her speech.

  o   Only the speaker's response time will be counted.

- **Yield to another delegate**: The speaker may yield his/her time to another delegate who supports their views.

  o   This gives the second delegate more time to elaborate on his/her ideas.

  o   When yielding to another delegate, be sure that the delegate whom you wish to yield the remaining time to is aware of your intentions beforehand, so they will not be caught unawares at the conclusion of your speech.

- **Yield to Comments**- A yield to comments allows two speakers, with thirty second speaking time each, to comment on the previous speech regardless of the remaining time.

  o   If a delegate fails to yield his/her remaining speaking time, their extraneous time will be donated to comments.

- A delegate would be ill-advised to yield his/her time in this manner.

Rights:

- **Right of Reply**- A delegate may rise upon this right if he/she has been personally offended, or feels that his/her country's dignity has been insulted.

    - Since this is serious action to take, a delegate should be wary to introduce such a right to the committee before he/she has certified just cause.

Rules of Procedure

Motion	Description	Vote	Requires Second	Debateable	Interrupt	Amendable
Adopt by Acclamation	Pass a draft resolution by consensus.	No	Yes	No	No	No
Adopt the Agenda	Sets the agenda.	Simple majority	Yes	No	No	Yes
Close the Speaker's List	Prevents delegates from being added to the speaker's list.	Simple majority	Yes	Yes	No	No
Open the Speaker's List	Allows delegates to be added to the speaker's list.	Simple majority	Yes	Yes	No	No
Set the Speaking Time	Establishes or revises delegate speaking time.	Simple majority	Yes	Yes	No	No

Incidental

Motion	Description	Vote	Requires Second	Debateable	Interrupt	Amendable
Appeal Decision	Challenge a decision, and overrule the Chair's ruling.	⅔ Majority	Yes	Pro/Con	Yes	No
Consider	Review a draft resolution as a whole.	Simple majority	Yes	No	No	No
Consider by Paragraph	Review a section of a draft resolution.	Simple majority	Yes	No	No	Yes
Division of Question	Separates a resolution by clause, so each clause may be considered individually.	Simple majority	Yes	No	No	Yes
Parliamentary Inquiry	A question, directed to the Chair, regarding a procedural definition.	Chair	No	No	Yes	No
Point of Information	Request information from the Chair or the speaker.	Chair	No	No	Yes	No

Incidental (continued)

Motion	Description	Vote	Requires Second	Debateable	Interrupt	Amendable
Point of Order	Address a breach of procedure or violation of the rules.	Chair	No	No	Yes	No
Reconsider	Reintroduce a matter that has been previously discussed.	⅔ Majority	Yes	Yes	Yes	No
Right of Reply	Response of personal or national defamation.	Chair	No	No	Yes	No
Suspension of the Rules	Set aside the agenda in order to address a relevant issue.	⅔ Majority	Yes	Chair	No	No
Withdrawal of Motion	Retraction of a motion from the agenda.	Majority	Yes	No	No	No

Privileged

Motion	Description	Vote	Requires Second	Debateable	Interrupt	Amendable
Adjourn	Ends the conference until the next year.	Simple majority	Yes	No	No	No
Orders of the Day	Compels committee to return to the agenda or schedule.	Simple majority	Yes	No	No	No
Point of Privilege	A request that addresses the rights or privileges or the committee or its members.	Chair	No	No	Yes	No
Recess	Temporarily releases committee.	Simple majority	Yes	No	No	Yes

Subsidiary

Motion	Description	Vote	Requires Second	Debateable	Interrupt	Amendable
Amend	Modify a previous motion.	Simple majority	No	Yes	No	Yes
Debate Limit/Extend	Modify the rules of debate in order to limit or extend a speaker's time.	⅔ Majority	Yes	No	No	No
Postpone	Postpone debate of a subject.	Simple majority	Yes	Yes	No	Yes
Previous Question	Immediately ends debate, so the committee can move into voting procedure.	Simple majority	Yes	No	No	No
Table (Lay On)	Temporarily set aside business.	⅔ Majority	Yes	Yes	No	Yes
Table (Take From)	Resume business that had previously been set aside.	⅔ Majority	Yes	No	No	No

What is the Speaker's List?

At a Model UN conference, the Speaker's List is the first platform by which you can share your views with the committee. By definition, the Speaker's List determines the sequence in which delegates will address the committee. Ultimately, however, the Speaker's List functions as elementary debate; providing students the opportunity to gradually move into formal debate.

Opening the Speaker's List is normally the first action delegates take. At the beginning of each conference, after roll has been taken and the agenda has been set, the Chair will ask for a motion to open the Speaker's List. Once this motion has been introduced to the committee, the delegates will vote on whether to open the Speaker's List. More than likely, your committee will open the Speaker's List after the first vote, but regardless of when your committee enacts the Speaker's List, its function and purpose will remain the same.

Joining the Speaker's List is quite simple, all you have to do is raise your placard. Additionally, any delegate may be added to the Speaker's List at any time. So, if you are not present when the list is initially opened, or you decide to speak at a later time, you may send a note to the Dias at any point during the conference, and you will be added to the docket.

That being said, it is recommended that each delegate sign up for the Speaker's List even if he/she does not have anything to say at the moment the list is opened. Due to the lengthy nature of this portion of debate (the list tends to be extremely long,) it normally takes a large portion of the conference to exhaust the list. Meaning that by the time the committee has moved to a topic you wish to speak about, you might not have a chance to address your delegates if your name is not already present on the list. Therefore, it is always best to sign up early. Even if you never find an issue to address or pertinent point to make, you can always read your position paper verbatim, or yield the time to another country, and give them the opportunity to speak.

The Speaker's List that is described above is the Main or First Speaker's List, but while it is the first list, it is not the last list. During the course of debate, when there are no other points or motions on the floor, the committee will automatically return the the Speaker's List. Therefore it is critical that the list is always populated; because if no countries are listed, or the Speaker's List is exhausted, the committee session will be forced to end, whether on-time or prematurely.

Things to remember when speaking in front of committee:
- Do not use personal pronouns. It is unprofessional to project your personal views onto your fellow delegates. Try to remember that you are

representing a country, not yourself. Your speech should not reflect your ideas or beliefs in any manner.

- Be respectful. You should not use the Speaker's List as a platform to berate other delegates.

- Be time conscious. Most Speaker's Lists' allow each delegate one minute to speak. The Chair will stop you when one minute has elapsed, so keep time in mind when you are writing your speech.

- You don't have to stay on topic. The Speaker's List is not meant to be structured. Ad lib! You can talk about whatever you want, as long as it is in good taste.

If I have one suggestion to impart on you, it would be this: Get on the Speaker's List. Take the leap! You will no doubt be apprehensive, especially if it is your first conference, but raise your placard anyway. This is the best environment to practice your public speaking skills, because you are not really you at a conference. You are a delegate from another county. Therefore, no one will be judging your speech, or your beliefs, because they are the ideals of a country; a country you may have no affiliation with beyond the conference. So, take the step. You might be surprised by how exhilarating public speaking can be. Either way, whether you enjoy your time at the microphone, or not, you will be grateful you challenged yourself. Not to mention that without addressing the committee, your fellow delegates will have no idea whether their country's views align with your country's views. Meaning that you definitely will not get the most out of your Model UN experience, and may not make the necessary connections to pass your resolution. Take it from someone who has been there. You want to get on that list. I did not raise my placard at my first conference, and I will regret it for the rest of my life. Do not join me in that regret. Raise your placard.

What is a Moderated Caucus?

Before we delve into the definition of a moderated caucus, let us discuss the benefits of motioning for a moderated caucus. Participating in a moderated caucus is similar to engaging in an expedited debate. This form of debate is informal, focused, and fast; thereby providing you, the delegate, the perfect opportunity to both voice your views on a specific aspect of the topic area, and hear other countries present their positions on the subject. This is the perfect opportunity to suss-out the countries with whom you wish to craft a resolution. A moderated caucus is a regular occurrence at a Model UN conference, not only because of their quick and focused nature, but because most delegates prefer to address the committee about a specific topic as a opposed to speaking about a broad concern. This commonality becomes far more frequent as the Speaker's List grows. Mostly because a delegate whose name is at the end of the list has a better chance of speaking on an issue if a moderated caucus is proposed, rather than waiting for a turn on the tedious Speaker's List.

Honestly, there is no better platform than through a moderated caucus to determine who shares your ideas and who would be a valuable contributor to the resolution you are hoping to write.

Now, on to the definition. A moderated caucus is one of two types of informal debate. During a moderated caucus, the Chair regulates the discussion. Delegates are recognized individually at the discretion of the Chair. The delegate who has the floor addresses the entire committee on a specific topic for a set amount of time, and then returns to his/her seat. To propose a moderated caucus, a delegate must establish a purpose for the caucus, a time limit, and a speaking time. After the proposal has been introduced, the committee must pass the motion for the moderated caucus to begin. If the required qualifications of a moderated caucus are not stated, the motion will be ruled dilatory by the Chair.

By now you probably have a grasp of the purpose and proceedings of a moderated caucus, so we will now delve into caucus etiquette. I know, that sounds intimidating and boring. Certainly many of you have been intimately acquainted with etiquette, whether through a cotillion class or through a scarring experience with your silverware at a formal family dinner. Well, take a breath. We are not going to discuss the acceptable way to cut your prosciutto-wrapped quail, or how to correctly sit in your chair. Instead, we will outline the information you need to know in order to caucus effectively.

- Listen. Observe what everyone in your committee says: other delegates, the chair, your gut. Do not block people out. It is imperative that you follow the flow of debate during the conference.

- Take notes. Who knows, you may want to propose another moderated caucus based on a subject Greece addressed. Jotting down relevant ideas or questions not only keeps you engaged in the discussion, but proves a useful tool when you are speaking to other delegates or writing your working paper.

- Be courteous. Do not call attention to the failures of other counties or delegates. Rather than mention past flaws, propose future solutions. No one wants to hear your negative remarks, and no one will want to join your country bloc if you make such statements.

- Be time-conscious. Try to hit the high points of your argument while you have the floor. Do not attempt to impart all your beliefs and proposals to the committee during the 45 seconds you are allotted to speak. Instead, use your speaking opportunity to highlight two or three specific beliefs or goals. If other countries agree with your values or align with your beliefs, they can always send you a note asking for further information, or approach you during an unmoderated caucus for a more in-depth discussion of your ideas.

- Follow-up with delegates. Once a delegate has finished speaking, send them a note. Whether it is a 'that was a really interesting speech, I would love to hear more about it,' or an 'I would like to meet during the next unmoderated caucus to discuss my ideas with you,' communicate with other delegates. This is the best way to create a diverse country bloc, and a strong draft resolution.

- Make connections. One of the best parts of attending a Model UN conference is making friends. Get to know the delegates in your committee, not just by their country's name, but personally. Ask them where they are from, their favorite subject in school, whatever comes to mind. More than likely, you will encounter the people you meet at a conference again, either at another conference, or later in life. So, take advantage of the opportunity, and solidify the friendships. You never know when they may come in handy.

- Enjoy yourself. No one else can improve your experience, only you can. Put a smile on your face, breathe, and relax. The purpose of Model UN is to teach students valuable skills in an engaging and undemanding way. This should not be an upsetting or stressful situation.

Whether you motion for a moderated caucus, or speak on one that has already begun, make sure you participate in a moderated caucus. This is the best way to voice your opinions to the committee, and listen to those of the other delegates. Not to mention that it is one of the most important aspects of a well-rounded, overall Model UN experience. So, participate! Otherwise, you will certainly miss out. Additionally, you will have no idea who to collaborate with, and the other countries in your committee will have no baring of your position on the topic area.

What is an Unmoderated Caucus?

During your time in committee, the unmoderated caucus will be the most motioned for proposal. Why is this form of debate so popular, you may ask? Honestly, the argument for this type of caucus varies depending on who you speak with. This is the case because there are so many benefits to the unmoderated caucus: each delegate develops a unique rationale based on their proclivity. Subsequently, due to the variety of positive factors, committees tend to spend half of their conference time in an unmoderated caucus.

Before we continue, you should probably learn the definition of an unmoderated caucus, so you can imagine the situation, and thereby the benefits. An unmoderated caucus is a form of informal debate (caucusing) during which the committee places formal business on hold. Allowing delegates to leave their seats, walk around, or leave the room; whatever they need to do. Although the Chair does not preside over the committee at this time, the subject of discussion should focus on business relevant to the topic area. Ultimately, an unmoderated caucus serves as a break, typically lasting five to fifteen minutes. While most delegates use this opportunity to collaborate with other countries and draft working papers, some committee members spend the time using the bathroom or getting a snack. No matter how you spend your unmoderated caucus, its function proves a well-deserved respite from the otherwise rigorous, punctilious nature of formal debate.

So, here are the reasons why an unmoderated caucus proves a staple in a committee session.

First of all, unmoderated caucuses are not regulated by the Chair. This gives delegates the freedom to walk around, meet with other countries, and begin drafting resolutions. Consequently, most of the other benefits of this form of debate stem from the temporary, laissez-faire supervision of the Chair.

Secondly, an unmoderated caucus is a great way to meet other delegates. The time during this unregulated debate is the perfect opportunity to converse with other countries, learn about different ideas, and begin forming country blocs.

Finally, participating in an unmoderated caucus provides delegates the best opportunity to work on resolutions. This proves true because of the fluidity of the unmoderated caucus. During this period of committee session, delegates are allowed to move around, split from previous country blocs, and form new coalitions. Due to this flexibility, delegates are free to focus on making connections and creating viable resolutions, rather than listening to the Chair or respecting the country presenting to the committee. These factors are crucial to completing a cohesive paper. Undoubtedly, the time your committee spends in an unmoderated caucus will prove useful in completing your document, no matter the status of your resolution.

Surely, there are many more reasons why unmoderated caucuses prove delegate favorites at a Model UN conference, and I hope you have the opportunity to discover a few on your own. Regardless of the reason for proposing an unmoderated caucus, the purpose remains steadfast: to provide delegates the opportunity to discuss issues, create country blocs, and draft resolutions. Although the committee does not technically have to be in an unmoderated caucus for delegates to accomplish the aforementioned tasks, an unmoderated caucus is certainly more conducive to a collaborative environment than any other form of debate, formal or informal.

Therefore, when you are sufficiently prepared to begin discussing the best solution to your topic area, or you need a quick break to grab an afternoon snack, propose an unmoderated caucus. Not only will you experience the excitement of proposing a motion, you will create the perfect opportunity to informally dialogue with other delegates; regardless of the reasoning behind the unmoderated caucus you request, your committee members will thank you.

How to Form a Country Bloc

Want to write a resolution with a group of like-minded, powerful countries? Then it is time to create/join a country bloc! Although joining a preexisting group of countries is great, creating your own circle of delegates can be even more meaningful. So, take the initiative early, get a group assembled, and get to work on your resolution! Still don't know where to start, or how to begin the process? Follow these ten simple rules and you will have a country bloc formed in no time!

1.   Come to the conference prepared. Have a solid understanding of your country's position on the topic area you are going to discuss in committee. Also, make sure you have a general idea of what you want to include in your resolution. Delegates want to associate with a strong leader with firm beliefs and a grasp on the goals they hope to accomplish during the conference.

2.   Start lobbying early. Approach delegates as soon as possible. Get the conference room before committee begins and start introducing yourself to other delegates. There is no such thing as creating a country bloc too fast.

3.   Put yourself out there. Give speeches, approach neutral countries, chat with the delegates in your committee, or anything else you can think of that will give you the opportunity to make your ideas known!

4.   Bring a computer. No one wants to hand-write a three page working paper, four page draft resolution, or five page resolution. If you are the smart delegate who brought a computer, people will line-up to contribute their opinions while you do all the typing. Seriously, if all else fails, be the one with the computer. Delegates will flock to you by the dozens.

5.   Make connections! Do your ideas align with those of Germany? Then talk to them! You do not have to agree with them on every issue to form a country bloc with a delegate. Seriously, when it comes to forming a group that will assist you with your resolution, the more the merrier.

6.   Establish a relationship with the person representing the country, not the country itself. Learn the names of the countries in your bloc. Sure, it might be easier to call people "United Kingdom" or "Norway," but it is much more appropriate to address delegates by their names. Taking the time to learn someone's name demonstrates your interest in those you interact with over your desire to pass a resolution. Learn those names, and delegates will feel connected to you, making them less likely to leave your bloc.

7.   Look for resourceful candidates. Once you have recruited a solid group of delegates, you will have to start assigning people to research past resolutions, write amendments, edit the document, recruit more members, and speak about the mission.

8.   Empower your allies. Representing the United States? Support your neighbor to the North, Canada. Seriously, make it your mission to bond with the delegates who represent the countries located near yours.

9.   Be open-minded. It is in your best interest to incorporate the views of as many countries as possible. Most resolutions wind up being combined by the end of the conference, so you might as well include some opinions you would otherwise disagree with. Otherwise, your resolution is less likely to be passed.

10.   Although approaching the countries that are located near you geographically is a great place to start, you don't have to form a country bloc with your country's "conventional allies." If Iran and the United states share the same opinion on the status of refugees, then it is perfectly acceptable for them to collaborate, or even craft a joint resolution.

Remember, this is not the (insert your name here) show. Model UN is about compromise and collaboration. You will not, and should not, count on getting your way on every issue. Take the time to listen to other delegates. Everyone in your committee (hopefully!) has spent hours researching their country and topic area. Listen to the opinions *and* concerns of other countries. Who knows, you might just learn something new, or better yet, form a new opinion.

Passing Notes: Is That Even Allowed?

You walk into your first committee session. The room is packed and booming with the voices of the hundred-plus boisterous, enthusiastic delegates at your conference. You want to approach your neighbor, Denmark, but before you have the chance to open your mouth, the Chair bangs the gavel and calls the committee to order. Sound familiar? Anyone who has been to a Model UN conference knows how difficult it is to talk to another delegate in a large committee. That is where passing notes comes in handy.

Yes, I know what you are thinking.

"At school when I pass a note to my friend, we get into trouble. Why is passing notes allowed at a Model UN conference?"

While it may be shocking that passing notes is allowed at first, after your first hour at a busy Model UN conference, you will understand why passing a note is the best way to communicate with other delegates.

Want to introduce yourself to another country? Want to comment on another country's speech? Want to invite another country to meet with your country bloc during the next unmoderated caucus? Pass them a note! Ultimately, you can pass notes for any reason you want, but here are some examples of the kinds of notes most delegates send in committee.

Appropriate Note Examples:

From: United Arab Emirates

To: China

Note: Hey UAE, what is your position on the illegal organ trade?

From: Algeria

To: Ethiopia

Note: Hey Ethiopia, I really enjoyed your speech about the spread of Malaria in Sub-Saharan Africa. Do you want to meet during the next unmoderated caucus?

From: India

To: Afghanistan

Note: Hey Afghanistan, are you working with the United Kingdom on the working paper regarding World Drug Trade?

From: Brazil

To: Chile

Note: Hey Chile, I think you would fit in really well to the country bloc I have started with Argentina. We would love to meet with you during the next unmoderated caucus.

From: China

To: Laos

Note: Hey Laos, could we meet during the next unmoderated caucus to discuss the spread of disease in third world countries?

Unfortunately, some delegates do not follow the note-passing rules, and send notes that are not relevant to the committee or topic area. Although I hope you aren't that person, I wanted to include some examples of inappropriate notes.

Inappropriate Note Examples:

From: Greenland

To: Switzerland

Note: Hey Switzerland, do you want to hang out after committee?

From: Australia

To: New Zealand

Note: Hey New Zealand, did you like my post on Instagram?

From: France

To: Spain

Note: Hey Spain, let's leave now and grab some coffee.

Things to Remember:

- Address the note to the country you wish to send it to and sign the note with your country's name.

    ○ Try to address the note on the outside, so you can fold the paper over and write your message on the inside.

    ○ If you don't address or sign the note, then the note will either never get to the delegate you addressed it to, or you will never receive a response because the recipient will have no idea to whom to send the note.

- Your notes should be clear, specific, and relevant.

- Make sure your note is legible.

- Pass a note to:

    ○ Ask a delegate to collaborate on a resolution.

    ○ Brainstorm ideas for resolutions.

    ○ Comment on a delegate's speech.

- Never write anything on a note that you wouldn't want your Grandma to read.

- When in doubt about the contents of your note, don't send it. Some Chairs dismiss the authors of inappropriate/irrelevant notes from committee.

Passing notes is a great way to get stuff done in committee and a fun way to talk to delegates in your committee! Just remember that passing notes in committee is a privilege and should be treated as such.

What is a Working Paper?

So, you have mastered the skills of debate, and you are ready to begin crafting a solution to the problem your committee is tasked to solve. That means you are ready to begin drafting a working paper, which is when the real Model UN experience begins.

A working paper serves as the precursor to a resolution. Since the goal of participating in a Model UN conference is to compose and pass a resolution, the working paper is essentially the first draft of said treatise.

Fundamentally, a working paper articulates the ideas of the committee members. It addresses the problem, asserts the necessary action steps, and highlights various points of contention in an effort to delineate a solution to a global issue.

Since the working paper merely serves as an outline, it does not have an established format. However, because a working paper is the first step to writing a resolution, most Chairs require that the paper be submitted in resolution format. While such a requirement may seem like a hassle at first, it will save a large amount of time when you decide to turn your working paper into a draft resolution. Although some conferences have an established format they want delegates to follow, the content of the working paper is far more important than its format, so do not become consumed by the outline, you can always alter the structure when you have concrete ideas.

In order to pen a successful working paper, you must be collaborative and flexible. Not every member of the committee will share the same ideas you have, so you must be prepared to listen to their ideas and compromise if need be in the interest of the committee. This is extremely important because a working paper may only contain signatories and cannot be voted upon, so your paper can only be approved at the discretion of a committee that is completely unfamiliar with your beliefs and ideas.

Once you have created a comprehensive and inclusive document, you are ready to submit your work to the Dias. After the Dias has reviewed your paper, they will either introduce it to your committee or reject the submission. If your work is approved, you will be given the opportunity to introduce your working paper and discuss your ideas with the delegates in your room. At this point, your document becomes a draft resolution.

Crafting such a paper may seem like a daunting task, but in reality it is quite simple. As long as you remember these tips, you will not only produce a stellar report, but you will also complete said paper in record time.

A working paper must be:

- inclusive. No one will pass your paper if the only people it benefits are you and a select group of delegates. Make sure you keep the views and values of other countries in mind when you compose your paper.

- practical. While radical working papers are entertaining to read, they rarely receive approval from the Dais or pass the committee. Keep your paper realistic and conservative.

- feasible. In conjunction with practicality, a working paper must be feasible. The point of the exercise that is a Model UN conference is to pretend that countries will actually adopt your ideas. It would be unwise to spend valuable time writing a resolution that would not be passed by the United Nations.

If you apply these tips to your working paper, you will be well on your way to creating an enviable piece of legislation.

Working Paper Template

Although you may use this template to construct your working paper, keep in mind that there is no strict format for a working paper. This merely serves as an example of one of the many possible formats one could use to compose a working paper.

Committee Name:

Working Paper Number:

Topic:

Signatories:

1   Problem facing the world

2

3   Actions that have been taken

4   a. contributing committee/organization

5   b. contributing committee/organization

6   c. contributing committee/organization

7   d. contributing committee/organization

8

9   Reason why the issue should be addressed

10

11   Hopes for the future

12

13   1. Step toward solution

14   a. sub-step

15

16   2. Step toward solution

17   a. sub-step

18   b. sub-step

19   c. sub-step

20

21   3. Step toward solution

22

23   Concluding sentence that highlights the necessity for such a resolution and
calls upon other delegates to contribute to the cause.

Example Working Paper

Committee Name: Disarmament and International Security

Working Paper Number: 1.3

Topic: Nuclear Proliferation

Signatories: China, France, Russia, United Kingdom, United States

1   The authors of this working paper believe that all other countries should stop

2   developing nuclear weapons. Therefore, we propose:

3

4   Every country that has developed nuclear weapons or other weapons of mass

5   destruction (WMD) should work to disband their programs.

6   Every country that is currently developing WMD will be placed on a watch
list,

7   and will be inspected each month for the first three years after the program is

8 implemented.

9 1. Recommending that country searches be conducted regularly.

10 2. Calling for the creation of a sub-committee of the Department of Safety

11 and Security (DSS) and will look for the following:

12   a. evidence of nuclear weapons or other WMD

13   b. active nuclear weapon or WMD development facilities

14   c. nuclear weapons or WMD that are being used for energy

15 2. Urges all member-states to contribute to the cause, and to stop nuclear

16 proliferation.

17 3. Suggests that all member-states educate themselves on the necessary response

18 to unapproved nuclear activity, and compelling nations to:

19   a. report unsavory actions

20   b. say something if you see something

21 4. Condemns all nations who support the spread of WMD and disregard the need

22 for international security.

23 5. These nations hope to improve the safety and security of the world with this document. Please supply suggestions as appropriate.

What is a Draft Resolution?

Once you're working paper has been approved, the next step in the resolution writing process is to craft a comprehensive draft resolution. As a whole, this document functions as an extended sentence, highlighting a problem, outlining necessary actions, and proposing a solution. Essentially, a draft resolution is a resolution that has not been voted on by the committee.

A delegate may write a draft resolution alone, or with the help of other member-states. More often than not, however, delegates compose draft resolutions with a bloc of other countries because a resolution proves more effective if it is born out of collaboration.

Divided into three parts, a draft resolution is similar to a position paper, organized by the: heading, preamble, and operative section.

The heading includes the committee name, draft resolution number, topic area, sponsors, and signatories. Ultimately, the heading functions to tell the committee members the subject of the resolution, who created the document, and who the resolution will affect.

The preamble describes the current state of the international community in regards to the issue. This section could reference committees that have already been formed in regards to addressing the issue, or it could include the various initiatives that have been developed in the hopes of resolving this issue. Essentially, this section refers to past programs in an effort to justify present action. In order to create a viable draft resolution, a delegate should utilize this section to reference a host of programs and past resolutions in order to supply their draft resolution with credibility.

The final piece of a draft resolution is the operative section. In this portion of the document, the action steps your committee is advised to take in order to resolve the issue are detailed. The operative section should be comprehensive and thorough, and should itemize the support and funding required to resolve the issue. A delegate should use this section to both address the procedures and outline the policies their resolution will establish.

A draft resolution is a wonderful way to alert your committee about a problem your country bloc hopes to resolve. Overall, a draft resolution is fairly simple to write, especially if you have the help of other delegates.

Although you should not face a problem writing your draft resolution, these suggestions will ensure you are on the right track. Make sure your draft resolution is:

- Collaborative. It is unlikely that the committee will be receptive to the work of an individual country. Try to include as many perspectives and countries as possible.

- Detailed. You do not want to propose a half-baked solution. Make sure you have both considered each aspect of your resolution and viewed the resolution as an entity.

- Original. Do not copy someone else's work or plagiarize a resolution that has already been debated in the United Nations. Not only is it illegal and morally corrupt, you will rob yourself of the experience of composing your own draft resolution.

- Easy to understand. While Model UN students tend to be quite bright, they do not want to spend valuable committee time deciphering your confusing musings or outlandish vocabulary choices. Make your document easy to read and write in plain English.

- Realistic. Similar to the working paper, you want to make sure your draft resolution is do-able. No one wants to debate an infeasible plan.

When your draft resolution is completed, you must search for signatories. Signatories are not required to support the entire draft resolution, but they must desire to see the idea debated. This is crucial to the success of your paper because before a draft resolution may be submitted to the Dias for consideration, it must have the support of twenty-percent of the committee. Additionally, many conferences have a minimum number of Sponsors that each resolution must obtain to be considered. Keep this in mind when you begin editing and combing your working papers.

Once your draft resolution is completed and you have garnered the support of twenty-percent of your peers, you may present your work to the Dias. After your draft resolution has been approved by the Chair, it will be formally introduced to the committee. This can be accomplished with a motion by one of the draft resolution's sponsors. After the motion has been made, the presenting sponsor will read the document to the committee and open the floor for discussion.

The debate that ensues will be intensive, as it will determine whether your committee agrees with your paper, and if your fellow delegates will pass or fail your resolution.

Draft Resolution Template

Committee Name:

Draft Resolution Number:

Topic:

Sponsors:

Signatories:

The (Committee Name),

1   *PREAMBULATORY PHRASE* (followed by a preambulatory clause),

2

3   *PREAMBULATORY PHRASE* (followed by a preambulatory clause),

4

5

6   *PREAMBULATORY PHRASE* (followed by a preambulatory clause),

7

8   1.   <u>OPERATIVE PHRASE</u> (followed by an operative clause):

9   a. Sub-clause;

10   b. Sub-clause:

11   i. (sub-sub-clause);

12   c. Sub-clause;

13   2.   <u>OPERATIVE PHRASE</u> (followed by an operative clause);

14   a. Sub-clause:

15   i. (sub-sub-clause);

16   ii. (sub-sub-clause);

17   iii. (sub-sub-clause);

18   iv. (sub-sub-clause);

19   3.   <u>OPERATIVE PHRASE</u> (followed by an operative clause):

20   a. Sub-clause;

21   b. Sub-clause;

22   4.   <u>OPERATIVE PHRASE</u> (followed by an operative clause).

Example Draft Resolution

Committee Name: United Nations Environment Programme

Draft Resolution Number: 2.2

Topic: Deforestation

Sponsors: China, India, Indonesia, Laos, Malaysia, Nepal, Philippines, Singapore, Thailand

Signatories: Andorra, Greece, Italy, Mexico, Portugal, United Kingdom

The United Nations Environment Programme,

1   *FULLY AWARE* that over 15 million hectares of forest were converted to other

2   uses or lost through natural events between 2000 and 2015, and

3   *ALARMED* that the Amazon has lost 15 percent of its forest cover since 1970,

4   predominantly for cattle ranches and small-scale subsistence agriculture, and

5   *KEEPING IN MIND* that climate change continues to affect deforestation, and

6   increase the side-effects and repercussions of such careless actions,

7   1.   <u>RECOMMENDS</u> that all countries:

8   a. Plant 100 trees for each cleared hectare;

9   b. Stop cutting down trees:

10   i. Unless for an approved project;

11   c. Invest in a more environmentally friendly way to increase revenue; and

12   2.   <u>URGES</u> each member-state to consider the importance of this issue; and

13   3.   <u>APPRECIATES</u> the environmental benefits these actions will bring; and

14   4.   <u>CONDEMNS</u> all nation-states who do not heed the warnings or participate

15   in the programs this sub-committee has created or will created in the

16   future; and

17   3.   <u>CONGRATULATES</u> all countries who help further the efforts to stop

18   deforestation, and thereby improve the state of the international

19   community.

Pre-ambulatory Phrases and Operative Clauses

Both pre-ambulatory phrases and operative clauses are used in the body of the resolution.

Pre-ambulatory phrases are used to explain the purpose of the resolution, describe the problem that is being addressed, and recall past actions taken to resolve the problem. Each clause of the preamble of the resolution begins with an italicized pre-ambulatory phrase and ends with a comma. Ultimately, these clauses offer support for the operative clauses that follow.

Pre-ambulatory clauses encompass:

- References to the Charter of the United Nations

- Citations of past resolutions or treaties enacted by the United Nations

- Elaboration on how nongovernmental or not-for-profit organizations have responded or are responding to the issue

- General statements on the significance and impact of the topic on regional communities, member states, and the United Nations as an entity

Affirming	Guided By
Alarmed by	Having adopted
Approving	Having considered
Aware of	Having examined
Bearing in Mind	Having heard
Believing	Having received
Cognizant of	Having studied
Confident	Keeping in mind
Contemplating	Noting further
Convinced	Noting with concern
Declaring	Noting with regret
Deeply concerned	Noting with satisfaction
Deeply convinced	Reaffirming
Deeply disturbed	Realizing
Deeply regretting	Recalling
Emphasizing	Recognizing
Expecting	Referring
Fulfilling	Seeking
Fully aware	Welcoming

Operative clauses offer solutions to issues addressed earlier in the resolution. These clauses state the action that is to be taken by the committee body. Tending to be more emotive than preambulatory clauses, operative clauses begin with underlined presence tense active verbs and end with a semicolon except for the final clause, which ends in a period.

Operative clauses express:

- What the signatories believe the committee should do to overhaul the issue

- Practical action steps that should be taken to resolve the problem

- Necessary rules and regulations

- The funding needed to achieve these goals

Accepts	Further recommends
Affirms	Further reminds
Approves	Further requests
Authorizes	Further resolves
Calls for	Has resolved
Calls upon	Notes
Confirms	Proclaims
Congratulates	Reaffirms
Considers	Recommends
Declares accordingly	Regrets
Deplores	Reminds
Designates	Requests
Emphasizes	Resolves
Encourages	Solemnly affirms
Endorses	Strongly condemns
Expresses its appreciation	Supports
Expresses its hope	Trusts

Further invites

Urges

Further proclaims

Welcomes

What is a Resolution?

A resolution is the reason why you attend a Model UN conference. It is the culmination of all your research, collaboration, and debate. Ultimately, your resolution is the final product of your time in committee.

Unfortunately, you can't just waltz into a conference and start scribbling out a position paper. There are steps that have to be followed, so you have to be patient. Don't become discouraged by the lengthy list of requirements and expectations! After you read this chapter, which will walk you through the steps each delegate must take before presenting his/her views, hopes, and goals to the committee, you will be prepared to tackle the resolution-writing process.

Steps to Take Before You Start Writing a Resolution:

    1.   Research possible solutions. Are there resolutions that the United Nations has already passed regarding your topic area? Great! Incorporate them into your own goals, or use them in your resolution.

2.   Outline the components of the topic area that you want to feature in your resolution.

3.   Form a Country Bloc.

4.   Ask countries to become Signatories and Sponsors of your resolution.

5.   Start writing your working paper.

6.   Revise your Working Paper.

7.   Submit your Working Paper to the Dias (when the motion is introduced to committee).

8.   Possibly combine your Working Paper with the Working Papers of other countries, if the views/goals are similar.

9.   Present your Working Paper to the committee.

10.   Begin working on your Draft Resolution (make sure you have enough Signatories and Sponsors to meet the requirements set by your conference for Resolution submissions).

11.   Revise your Draft Resolution.

12.   Submit your Draft Resolution.

13.   Possibly combine your Draft Resolution with the Draft Resolution of other countries, if the views/goals are similar.

14.   Present your Draft Resolution to the committee.

15.   Begin working on your Resolution.

16.   Remember: Resolution lengths may vary, so do not worry if you think yours seems too long or too short.

Now, let's move on to the process of writing a resolution. However, before we outline the steps a delegate must go through to complete such a document, keep in mind that this paper is the edited, revised, and polished solution to the problem your committee was tasked to solve. Do not give your resolution a negative tone, or make any disparaging or defaming remarks about any country in the document. Above all, a resolution is an assemblage of the hard-work and ideas of your committee, so be sure it conveys that passion. On a formatting note, remember that a resolution is made up of three parts: the heading, the preambulatory clauses, and the operative clauses.

Steps to Writing a Strong Resolution:

1.   Begin with the heading. Write your committee name, resolution number, topic area, sponsors, and signatories at the top left hand corner of the page. If you want to be really fancy, you can also include the date of the conference.

2.   Then, preface your proposal. Write, "The (insert committee name here) would like to propose a resolution to the problem (insert topic area here).

3.   Next, the preambulatory clauses. Always begin a preambulatory clause with a preambulatory phrase (which should be italicized) and end it with a comma. The purpose of the preambulatory clauses is to state the issues that the resolution is meant to solve. These clauses basically answer the why and when questions regarding the topic area. Keep in mind that most resolutions have three to five preambulatory clauses. Preambulatory clauses can include:

   a.   A short description of the problem, its impact, or its relevance.

   b.   A quick reference to the United Nations Charter (if relevant).

   c.   Previous meetings, treaties, or actions held by the United Nations in regards to the issue you hope to resolve.

   d.   Prior local, regional, or national efforts dealing with said problem.

4.   Operative clauses come next. Operative clauses should be numbered in chronological order. Always begin an operative clause with an operative phrase (which should be underlined) and end it with a semicolon. An operative clause states the solution(s) proposed in a resolution. Try to ensure that the operative clauses you include are in reference to your preambulatory clauses.

5.   If you have more to say about an operative clause, you can end your sentence with a colon and add an operative sub-clause. Operative sub-clauses are especially helpful if you don't have enough room to say what you want in the space an operative clause provides.

6.   You are done! Great work, end your resolution with a period and click print.

7.   Use the resolution template and review the example resolution, if need be, and prepare to learn about the beauty of friendly and unfriendly amendments.

Resolution Template

Committee Name:

Resolution Number:

Topic:

Sponsors:

Signatories:

The (Committee Name),

1   *PREAMBULATORY PHRASE* (followed by a preambulatory clause),

2

3   *PREAMBULATORY PHRASE* (followed by a preambulatory clause),

4

5

6   *PREAMBULATORY PHRASE* (followed by a preambulatory clause),

7

8   1.   OPERATIVE PHRASE (followed by an operative clause):

9   a. Sub-clause;

10   b. Sub-clause;

11   c. Sub-clause;

12   d. Sub-clause;

13   2.   OPERATIVE PHRASE (followed by an operative clause):

14   a. Sub-clause:

15   i. (sub-sub-clause);

16   3.   OPERATIVE PHRASE (followed by an operative clause):

17   a. Sub-clause:

18   i. (sub-sub-clause);

19   ii. (sub-sub-clause);

20   b. Sub-clause;

21   c. Sub-clause;

22   4.   OPERATIVE PHRASE (followed by an operative clause).

Example Resolution

Committee Name: Disarmament and International Security Committee

Resolution Number: 3.1

Topic: Nuclear, Biological, and Chemical weapon proliferation

Sponsors: Albania, Australia, Poland, Russia, Spain, Switzerland, United Kingdom, United States

Signatories: Argentina, Colombia, Greece, Iceland, Norway, Seychelles, Sweden

The Disarmament and International Security Committee,

1   *RECALLING* the treaty on the nonproliferation of nuclear weapons (NPT) that

2   the United Nations reviewed in 1995,

3   *ALARMED* by the proliferation of nuclear, biological and chemical weapons

4   since the creation of the aforementioned treaty,

5   *DEEPLY CONCERNED* by the countless lives lost due to the spread of nuclear,

6   biological, and chemical weapons,

7   *CONFIDENT* that the international community can once again come together to

8   solve this pressing problem by following a few simple steps,

9   1. <u>CALLS</u> all non-signatories be urged to adopt the Nuclear Non-Proliferation

10   Treaty;

11   2. <u>ENCOURAGES</u> each member-state take action to reduce their respective

12   nuclear stockpiles and stop developing biological and chemical weapons:

13   a. Hoping to affirm a safer world in the future;

14   b. Understanding the benefits of a nuclear-free world;

15   3. <u>RECOMMENDS</u> that the United Nation establish nuclear-free-zones within

16   the borders of each member-state;

17   4. <u>RECOGNIZES</u> the importance of nuclear energy, and understands the need

18   for continued development in field of nuclear energy;

19   5. <u>URGING</u> countries to adopt the resolution and thereby foster a safer

20   environment where nuclear energy research can be conducted without the threat 21   of terrorism.

What are Friendly and Unfriendly Amendments?

Once your draft resolution is approved, it can be altered by members of your committee. That is where friendly and unfriendly amendments come in.

Both friendly and unfriendly amendments are ways to enhance a resolution. These amendments can delete, revise, or supplement a resolution before said resolution is voted upon. Delegates make suggestions based on the grammar, content, or position of a resolution in order to make it a more compelling, inclusive, and well-rounded document. Ultimately, the amendment process is meant to be a positive experience.

A friendly amendment is a revision that is supported by the author and co-sponsors of the resolution. In other words, if the author or co-sponsors wish to alter their resolution, they propose a friendly amendment. Since these revisions are penned by the author(s) of a resolution, once friendly amendments are submitted to the Dias, they are applied to the resolution without debate or stipulation.

An unfriendly amendment is a revision that is not proposed by the author of a resolution. Most of the time, unfriendly amendments are supported by the sponsors and benign in nature, however, sometimes such alterations are not supported by the delegates who created the original document. After an unfriendly amendment is proposed, there is one speaker for and one speaker against the alteration. Following the pro/con debate, the committee votes on whether to incorporate the amendment into the body of the resolution. The vote must be a simple majority for the amendment to be approved.

As we have discussed throughout this book, Model UN is about collaboration. Which is what friendly and unfriendly amendments are in a nutshell. These revisions are just a more formal version of edits you would make to a paper, suggestions you would get from a teacher, or corrections you would receive from a friend. So do not be afraid to make friendly amendments to your resolution, and do not be offended if delegates in your committee introduce an unfriendly amendment. This is not an indictment of your writing ability or the strength of your argument. Take an unfriendly amendment as a complement. It proves that delegates have actually read your work, are interested in what you have to say, and are invested in your resolution. Chances are that they just want to make your resolution stronger.

How do I get My Resolution Passed?

With your resolution written, amendments introduced, and the end of the conference near you are probably ready to see your resolution passed. By now, most of the country blocs in your committee will have merged and the working papers you debated will be unrecognizable after being revised so many times. That said, it is highly probable that your committee will only have two or three resolutions on the table, instead of the dozens of papers you discussed at the beginning of the conference. Which means you have less competition for passing your resolution, right? Right. But you still face one hurdle, convincing your committee to adopt the document you have meticulously crafted. Seriously, how *do* you get your resolution passed?

All in good time, my friend.

While there are many tactics that can be used to get a resolution passed, there is no guaranteed way to win the votes of the delegates in your committee. This is due to the fact that every delegate, committee, and conference is unique. Keep that in mind when you are talking to other delegates and writing your document.

Even though there is no "resolution formula" to follow, you can still try these five tactics to get that simple, or two-thirds, majority you need!

1.   Be perceptive. Know your audience. That means talking to the delegates in your committee. What do they want to pass? Do they think it is a good idea to spend $15 billion dollars on mosquito nets to resolve the malaria problem in Sub-Saharan Africa? If they don't, then you should not included it in your resolution. Remember: even if your argument is bulletproof and your prose is skillfully crafted, if people are not responding to your resolution it is unlikely it will be approved.

2.   Be inclusive. Just because you think your ideas are the best does not mean you should be the sole author of your document. You can never have too many people in your country bloc. Persuade others to join your group by allowing them to include their ideas in your resolution. If you collaborate, compromise, and create relationships your resolution will be sure to pass. Seriously, Model UN is not the time to be selfish.

3.   Make friends. If you know someone personally, or as well as you can in the short time you are at a conference, they will be more likely to tell other delegates about your ideas and approve your resolution.

4.   Spread the message. Be vocal! Make speeches! Talk to people outside that committee room. The more people hear the name of your resolution and what it contains, the more likely they will be to vote "yay" instead of "nay."

5.   Combine. If all else fails, before the committee goes into voting procedure, combine with a resolution that your committee seems to like. Even

though you are not the original author of the document, at least you can say your resolution passed. This is completely acceptable in Model UN, as it is an example of one of the key cornerstones of a conference: collaboration.

Fortunately, most delegates want every resolution to pass, whether they are genuinely interested in your work or they want their own resolutions to be passed. Which bodes well for you and your document. Also, since a committee can pass as many resolutions as it desires, you are more likely to see your resolution approved.

Do not freak out if your resolution is not passed. Just remember that the purpose of participating in a Model UN conference is not to win, it is to learn. Actually, especially if it is your first conference, it is better if your resolution is not passed. Why, you ask? If your resolution fails, you are more likely to attend another conference, and then another, and another, until you eventually fall in love with Model UN.

So try these tactics, and if they do not work for you the first time, in the committee you are in, with the delegates you work with, do not have a panic attack. Instead, go home, sign up for another conference, and try again.

Congratulations! You Just Participated in Your First Model UN Conference

At this point you have either completed the book, skipped to the end, or just concluded your first conference. Regardless of which scenario it is, congratulations!

Now that you finished the book, you are probably thinking, "What do I do now?"

Well, you have several options.

1. Sign up for your first/next conference!

2. Re-read the book. Because you obviously cannot get enough of Model UN or me ;)

3. Take a nap.

4. Go on a walk with your mom.

5. Finish your homework.

6. Take out the garbage for your mom.

7. Start a Model UN conference at your school.

8.	Practice your skills by researching a country/topic area that interests you.

9.	Organize a Model UN conference at your school.

10.	Go to another Model UN conference and show everyone how good you are at parliamentary procedure. Seriously, you have spent enough time studying, reviewing, and preparing, strut your stuff!

Whatever you decide to do with your new knowledge of caucusing, debating, and parliamentary procedure, I am confident you will do it well. I am honored to have guided you through the process, and I am so happy that you have started your journey (and begun your obsession) with Model UN.

Go forth, my MUNers! Great debate, tremendous joy, and newfound relationships are just around the corner. I feel relieved that the future of our world will be bright because you will be the ones shaping it.

I look forward to seeing you guys at conferences and reading about your work in the coming years as you assume the roles of United Nations ambassadors, international business people, humanitarian activists, and countless other positions.

All my love,

-𝒱

Final Tips and Tricks

- Go in with an open mind. Model UN could be one of the best experiences of your life, it has been for me, but it certainly will not be if you go into a conference in the wrong mind-set. Caucusing and writing resolutions will be much easier if you are receptive to interesting perspectives, new ideas, or different values. And, you never know what you might learn if when you check your preconceived notions at the door.

- Be positive. In Model UN, and in life, no one wants to be around a negative person. Try your best to exude confidence, happiness, and warmth.

- Be forgiving. Everyone is a little shaky at their first conference, and some seasoned delegates are even a bit nervous for the first few hours of a the conference. We have all been there. Remember that when you want to call someone out for their use of parliamentary procedure.

- Be prepared. I know of no easier way to make a friend than by offering them a sharpened pencil or sheet of blank paper. Want to be that person in your committee? Bring a binder full of research materials, articles, and relevant information (for yourself). And, bring a respectable supply of blank paper (for your future buddies). Your preparation will not go to waste.

• Don't wing it. Smart delegates prepare speeches. You are a smart delegate, therefore you should prepare speeches. Take my advice, speaking extemporaneously is not attractive.

• Dress appropriately. Under no circumstances should you be wearing a mini skit to a Model UN conference. The same goes for you, boys! It is just easier to point out female fashion faux-pas. A nice blazer, skirt or slacks, and a blouse are appropriate garments for ladies. A nice sport coat, button-down shirt, and dress pants are acceptable for gentlemen.

• Start caucusing early. It is never too soon to show up to committee. Okay, four hours before the start time might be a little excessive, but A for effort you go-getter, you! Socializing before the conference begins goes along with being prepared and friendly. Talk to other delegates! Share your enthusiasm! Learn about their positions! That is why you go to a conference, after all.

• Be a good listener. Listen to your Chair. Listen to the delegates in your committee. Listen to your gut, but not too closely, people might think you are a bit off.

• Be respectful of other delegates. Even if you don't agree with someone. Even if you are offended by someone. Even if the person you seemingly 'just met' has morphed into your nemesis. There is no reason to stoop to their level. Hear the sing-songy voice your parents used when they told you to share your candy when you were a child, yet? I thought so.

• Do not assume your ideas are correct. Don't be pompous or arrogant in committee. I promise, no one will want to work with you. Instead, be adaptable and flexible. And remember, it is okay to admit you were wrong about something. We have all been there.

- Ask for help. Don't know how to motion for an unmoderated caucus? No problem! Ask the Chair how to use parliamentary procedure to correctly motion for an unmoderated caucus. Very few people know how to use parliamentary procedure perfectly. So don't be embarrassed if you don't know how to say something! Model UN is about learning, and the Chairs are always mostly happy to help!

- Speak up! Make it a personal goal to speak at least once in committee. First of all, you will be bored just sitting silently in committee. Secondly, no one will want to talk to you if you don't speak up. Finally, if you don't contribute to the discussion, you will definitely not get your money's worth from the conference.

- Be an engaging speaker. Talk to your audience. Appeal to their emotions. Relate to them. No one wants to listen to someone read from a note card in a monotoned voice.

- Believe in yourself. Take that risk. You are amazing!

- Challenge opinions. You aren't always right, and neither are the delegates in your committee. Do not be embarrassed to call someone out on a flaw in their argument or something you find hinky about their reasoning.

- Focus on making friends instead of passing your resolution. I cannot emphasis this enough! The connections you make at a conference are the most important part of Model UN.

- Use the third person when you are making motions. This is basic parliamentary procedure. Never use first person pronouns and you will be safe from bloodthirsty delegates who want to call you out in committee.

- If all else fails, and trust me, I have had my share of failures and slip-ups, just sit back, smile, and get as much as you can from the experience.

- Reference this book if you have a problem!

Testimonials

"I joined Model UN because I needed an after school credit. I thought it would be very boring, but it ended up being really fun. Participating in Model UN has has taught me a lot of things, including how the United Nations works and how to research for projects. I am really glad I tried Model UN." -- Joseph Longwell, sophomore at Heritage Hall.

"Although I did not know Parliamentary Procedure, I had a lot of fun at the Harvard Conference. I learned a tremendous amount about women's issues across the globe, as well as helping try to solve them. I enjoyed meetings and all of the other students involved. Traveling provided a very valuable and important experience for our team. I am very proud to call myself a part of Heritage Hall MUN, and I am excited to see where they go in the future." -- Carly Mirabile, freshman at Duke University.

"I enjoyed MUN, it was interesting to observe the different viewpoints of certain countries. Debate is an integral part of MUN, so by not being a great debater, it is better to observe and work on resolutions rather than actually speaking, though by observing a few speakers you could potentially learn the ropes. Anyway, I would most definitely recommend MUN to anyone looking for a potential career in politics. MUN is a great opportunity to meet new people from different schools and share ideas about impending issues around the globe." -- Marissa Wilson, senior at Heritage Hall.

"My overall experience with Model UN was amazing. I had lots of fun and made some friends at the conference I attended. Since I had such a positive experience, I've been trying to convince my friends to join because I know they will enjoy it." -- Matthew Ring, sophomore at Heritage Hall.

"I really enjoyed my MUN experience. I loved getting to go to the conference and meet people from all around the world. I learned a lot during the committee sessions and would definitely recommend the experience to others." --Paige Miles, senior at Heritage Hall.

"What an experience. As someone who is reasonably new to model UN, I wasn't quite sure what to expect or what I was getting into. That's how it turned out, it was the best choice I've made all year. The experience I had and the things I learned pertaining to global affairs and foreign-policy are invaluable and will stay with me throughout my college career and beyond." --Virinchi Sindhwani, freshman at the University of Southern California.

Example Conference Script

Dais: Will all the delegates please take their seats, the rapporteur will begin roll call momentarily.

Delegates sit.

Dais: Thank you, delegates. Welcome to the Legal Committee at the Model UN of the Southwest Conference. This committee session is now in order. My name is Vivian and I will be your Chair. This is my partner, Edward, he will be the Director of this committee. For those of you unaware of the roles of the Chair and Director, the Chair fields questions about the Rules of Procedure, while the Director addresses more specific questions about your country's foreign policies. Please feel free to write notes at any time during our sessions. You may address them to either your fellow delegates, or the Dais. Once you have written a note, please pass it to the volunteer pages circulating the room. We will open this committee session with roll call. When your country's name is called there are two appropriate responses: 'present' or 'present and voting.'

Delegates who answer 'present and voting' are not permitted to abstain from any substantive

vote, and must vote in favor or in opposition to any motion before the committee.

Roll is taken and the status of each delegate is recorded.

Dais: For those delegates who may have arrived while roll was being taken, people send a note to the Dais, so we can mark your attendance and voting status. Now that roll has been called, we will establish quorum. Quorum is the minimum number of consenting delegates required for the committee to conduct business. It is established to prevent any unrepresentative action that could be made in the name of this committee. Ultimately, quorum is 50% of the committee plus one delegate. Based on the attendance sheet, the quorum of this committee session will be 64 delegates. That means that in order for motions to pass, at least 64 delegates must both be present and vote in favor of the movement. Are there any motions on the floor at this time?

Delegates may raise their placard to signal they have a motion to make.

Dais: Seeing no motions on the floor at this time, we will open the Speaker's List for the purpose of setting the agenda. All those who wish to be placed on the Speaker's List should raise their placards.

The Chair will recognize countries while the Rapporteur records the order.

Dais: "If any additional countries wish to be added to the Speaker's List, please send a note to the Dais. Are there any points or motions on the floor at this time?"

The United States raises their placard.

Dais: "Delegate from the United States, on what point or motion do you rise?"

United States: "Motion to set the speaking time to one minute."

Dais: "That motion is in order. Are there any other point or motions on the floor at this time?"

Dais: "Seeing none, we will now vote on the motion. Just a reminder, this motion will only pass if there are 64 votes in favor. All delegates in favor of this motion?"

Delegates raise their placards and the Rapporteur records the votes.

Dais: "All those opposed?"

Delegates raise their placards and the Rapporteur records the votes.

Dais: "This motion passes. The speaking time is now set to one minute. Delegates who do not use the entire minute may yield the remaining time to the Chair, questions, or another delegate."

Five delegates speak. The delegate from China raises her placard.

Dais: "The delegate of China, on what point or motion do your rise?"

China: "Honorable Chair, China moves that we set the agenda in the following order: Topic Area B as the first topic to be addressed by the committee, and Topic Area A as the second topic to be addressed by the committee."

Dais: "Thank you, delegate. A motion has been made to set the committee agenda as follows: Topic Area B as the first topic to be addressed by the committee, and Topic Area A as the second topic to be addressed by the committee. Are there any further motions on the floor at this time?"
Germany raises his placard.

Dais: "Delegate from Germany, on what point or motion do you rise?"

Germany: "Honorable Chair, Germany moves that we set the agenda in the following order: Topic Area A as the first topic to be addressed by the committee, and Topic Area B as the second topic to be addressed by the committee."

Dais: "Thank you, delegate. A motion has been made to set the committee agenda as follows: Topic Area A as the first topic to be addressed by the committee, and Topic Area B as the second topic to be addressed by the committee. Are there any further motions on the floor at this time?"

Dais: "There are two motions on the floor at this time for the adoption of the agenda order, are there any additional motions on the floor at this time? Seeing no other points or motions, the committee will consider the first motion for the adoption of the agenda order. The order is as follows: Topic Area B as the first topic to be addressed by the committee, and Topic Area A as the second topic to be addressed by the committee. This motion is decided by a simple majority vote, and there is no debate required. All those in favor of this motion, please raise your placards.

Delegates raise their placards and the Rapporteur records the votes.

Dais: "All those opposed."

Delegates raise their placards and the Rapporteur records the votes.

Dais: "By a vote of 67 to 59, this motion passes. The agenda order, Topic Area B as the first topic to be addressed by the committee, and Topic Area A as the second topic to be addressed by the committee, has been adopted. The committee will now move into substantive session to address Topic Area B. Will those delegates who wish to be placed on the Speaker's List for the topic, please raise your placards.

The Speaker's List is opened and delegates raise their placards to be placed on the list.

Dais: "The delegate from Belgium is recognized for one minute."

The Speaker's List continues for about ten minutes.

Dais: "Seeing that we have been using the Speaker's List for about ten minutes, the Chair would entertain a motion for a moderated caucus. Are there any points or motions on the floor at this time?"

The delegate from Denmark raises her placard.

Dais: "Delegate from Denmark, on what point or motion do you rise?"

Denmark: "Honorable Chair, Denmark motions for a twelve minute moderated caucus with a 45 second speaking time on the subject of funding water wells in Sub-Saharan Africa."

Dais: "That is in order. Are there any other points or motions on the floor at this time?"

No one raises their placard.

Dais: "Seeing none, we will vote on the motion for a twelve minute moderated caucus with a 45 second speaking time on the subject of funding water wells in Sub-Saharan Africa. All those in favor of this motion, please raise your placard."

Delegates raise their placards and the Rapporteur records the votes.

Dais: "All those opposed."

Delegates raise their placards and the Rapporteur records the votes.

Dais: "By a vote of 91 to 35, this motion passes. We will now begin the twelve minute moderated caucus with a 45 second speaking time on the subject of funding water wells in Sub-Saharan Africa. If you would like to speak on this issue, please raise your placard after each delegate has finished speaking, and the Chair will recognize you. The delegate from Denmark has the floor."

The delegate from Denmark speaks and the moderated caucus continues.

Dais: "The time for this moderated caucus has elapsed. Are there any other points or motions on the floor?"

Japan: "Honorable Chair, the delegate from Japan would like to motion to extend the moderated caucus on the subject of funding water wells in Sub-Saharan Africa by five minutes."

Dais: "Thank you, delegate. That motion is in order. Is there a second to the motion for an extension of the moderated caucus on the subject of funding water wells in Sub-Saharan Africa by five minutes? "

Argentina: "Second."

Dais: "All delegates in favor of this motion to extend the moderated caucus on the subject of funding water wells in Sub-Saharan Africa by five minutes, please raise your placards."

Delegates raise their placards and the Rapporteur records the votes.

Dais: "All those opposed."

Delegates raise their placards and the Rapporteur records the votes.

Dais: "This motion passes. We will extend the moderated caucus on the subject of funding water wells in Sub-Saharan Africa by five minutes."

The moderated caucus continues for five minutes more.

Dais: "The time for this moderated caucus has elapsed. At this time the Chair would entertain a motion for an unmoderated caucus."

The delegate of Finland raises his placard.

Dais: "Delegate from Finland, on what point or motion do you rise?"

Finland: "Honorable Chair, Finland motions for a fifteen minute unmoderated caucus to discuss working papers."

Dais: "Thank you, delegate. That motion is in order. Is there a second to the motion for for a fifteen minute unmoderated caucus to discuss working papers.? "

Canada: "Second."

Dais: "All delegates in favor of a fifteen minute unmoderated caucus to discuss working papers, please raise your placards."

Delegates raise their placards and the Rapporteur records the votes.

Dais: "All those opposed."

Delegates raise their placards and the Rapporteur records the votes.

Dais: "This motion passes. We will now break for a fifteen minute unmoderated caucus to discuss working papers. Please keep your voices down as there are other committees still in session, and remember to be back in the committee room in fifteen minutes."

The delegates break for a fifteen minute unmoderated caucus.

Dais: "Welcome back, delegates. Are there any points or motions on the floor at this time?"

The delegate from Russia raises her placard.

Dais: "Delegate from Russia, on what point or motion do you rise?"

Russia: "Honorable Chair, Point of Personal Privilege, the delegates in the back of the room cannot hear the Turkish delegation."

Dais: "Thank you, delegates. Delegates, please make sure you project your voice when your address the committee. Are there any other points or motions on the floor at this time?"

The delegate from Thailand raises her placard.

Dais: "Delegate from Thailand, on what point or motion do you rise?"

Thailand: "Honorable Chair, Point of Parliamentary Inquiry, what is the next event on the agenda?"

Dais: "Thank you, delegate. The next item on the agenda is to vote on draft resolution 2.1. Are there any point or motions on the floor at this time?"

The delegate from Syria raises her placard.

Dais: "Delegate from Syria, on what point or motion do you rise?"

Syria: "Honorable Chair, Syria moves to close debate."

Dais: "Thank you, delegate. That motion is in order. Are there any other points or motions on the floor at this time?"

The delegate from Spain raises his placard.

Dais: "Delegate from Spain, on what point or motion do you rise?"

Spain: "Honorable Chair, Spain moves for adjournment of debate."

Dais: "Thank you, delegate. That motion is in order. Currently, there are two motions on the floor: one motion for the closure of debate and one motion for adjournment of debate. Are there any other points or motions on the floor at this time?"

No delegates raise their placards.

Dais: "Seeing none, the committee will consider the motions on the table. The committee will address the motion for the closure of debate first. This motion requires two speakers in opposition and is decided by a two-thirds majority vote. Before we open the floor to the opposing speakers, please keep in mind that the passage of this motion will formally end debate on this topic and the committee will immediately move into voting procedure. Any working papers that have not been formally introduced to the committee and approved by the Chair will not be eligible for consideration. Are there any questions regarding this motion?"

No delegates raise their placards.

Dais: "Seeing none, will the delegates who wish to speak in opposition to this motion for the closure of debate please raise their placards?"

Two delegates are selected, and are allowed fifteen seconds each to speak against the motion.

Dais: "The committee will now move into formal voting procedure on the motion. During voting procedure, no other motions can be accepted. We will now vote on the motion to close debate. This motion requires a two-thirds majority vote. Delegates who are in favor of this motion please raise your placards."

Delegates raise their placards and the Rapporteur records the votes.

Dais: "All those opposed."

Delegates raise their placards and the Rapporteur records the votes.

Dais: "By a vote of 86 to 40, this motion for the closure of debate passes. Having moved to close debate, the committee is now in formal voting procedure. We will now consider the two draft resolutions before the committee: draft resolution 1.3 and draft resolution 2.1. The Chair has not received any amendments to this draft resolution, so we will move directly into voting procedure. During voting procedure, note passing privileges will be suspended, you will not be permitted to leave the room."

The delegate from Nigeria raises her placard.

Dais: "Delegate from Nigeria, on what point or motion do you rise?"

Nigeria: "Honorable Chair, Nigeria moves to adopt this resolution by acclamation."

Dais: "Thank you, delegate. That motion is in order. A motion has been made to adopt draft resolution 1.3 by acclamation. A motion to pass a resolution by acclamation signifies that the committee is in consensus as to the contents of the draft resolution. Is there any opposition to the motion to adopt draft resolution 1.3 by acclamation?"

No delegates raise their placards.

Dais: Seeing no opposition to this motion, the draft resolution 1.3 is adopted by the consensus decision of the committee and officially becomes Resolution 1.1."

The committee applauds the passage of the first resolution.

Dais: "The second, and final, draft resolution before the committee is draft resolution 2.3. There are no amendments to this draft resolution. So, seeing no motions on the floor at this time, we will move to vote on draft resolution 2.3. Will all those delegates in favor of draft resolution 2.3 please raise their placards. "

Delegates raise their placards and the Rapporteur records the votes.

Dais: "All those opposed."

Delegates raise their placards and the Rapporteur records the votes.

Dais: "By a vote of 100 in favor, 20 opposed, and 6 abstentions, draft resolution 2.3 is adopted by the committee and is now Resolution 1.2."

The committee applauds the passage of the second resolution.

Dais: "With the passage of the final resolution, this committee has concluded debate on the first topic area. We will now move into the second topic area. We will now open the Speaker's List for this topic area."

Debate continues with the second topic area.

Once debate on the second topic area has concluded, the committee will be prepared for adjournment of the meeting.

The delegate from Australia raises his placard.

Dais: "Delegate from Australia, on what point or motion do you rise?"

Australia: "Honorable Chair, Australia motions for the Adjournment of this meeting."

Dais: "Thank you, delegate. That motion is in order. All those in favor of this motion to adjourn the meeting please raise your placard."

Delegates raise their placards and the Rapporteur records the votes.

Dais: "All those opposed."

Delegates raise their placards and the Rapporteur records the votes.

Dais: "This motion passes. This Model UN committee is now adjourned. Thank you, delegates for your composure and decorum throughout this committee session. I hope to see you all next year!"

Acknowledgements

Most of you know her as Catherine Armitage, but I know her as mom. She has taught me everything I know, from creating neverending to-do lists, to buying fresh fish, to baking the perfect potato. All of my profitable skills were learned from this woman. She is my biggest supporter and my greatest inspiration; everything I have done, and everything I aspire to accomplish is thanks to her. Although I tend to become annoyed by her persistent nagging and overwhelming to-do lists, she will always have my unconditional love. Mom, you are the best cheerleader. Thank you for your devotion. I love you, and I will always be your mini-me.

My daddy, John Armitage, for encouraging me to pursue entrepreneurial adventures. You are the best example of a man who is in love with his carrer; your desire to share the gift of life is infectious. Thank you for your wisdom and guidance, for showing me that it is alright to take risks, and for teaching me the proper way to eat french fries: with a sweet and tangy mustard-and-ketchup mixture. I am eternally grateful for all the lessons and stories you shared with me.

My brother, Elliott Armitage, for putting up with all my worksheets, questionnaires, and exercises. You were the best guinea pig a girl could ask for. Thank you for being my friend, playmate, and confidant. Your energy, creativity, and imagination are delightful. Even when your stubbornness and histrionics put us in opposition, I still love you. I hope you never lose your spark.

My Papa, Edward Elliott. You were the most charismatic, jubilant man I have ever met. You brought light into the lives of everyone you met. Your interminal ability to converse with reserved waiters, put standoffish cashiers at ease, and bring smiles to the faces of the exhausted diner denizen was astounding. I aspire to ask as many people 'where are you from?' as you did. Thank you for imparting the importance of listening to other people's stories.

Cassie Eads and Chris Elliott. Thank you for believing in a short, shy high school freshman, for pretending you thought my idea would work, and for masking your amazement when it actually succeeded. I will never be able to adequately thank you for your support. Cassie, you are the most encouraging mentor I could have ever dreamed of. Thank you for all the recommendation letters you have written for me, and the confidence you have in my ideas, no matter how outlandish.

Zach Sumner, my tutor. Thank you for agreeing to educate me. You are always willing to embark on new adventures in learning; and always manage to quench my thirst for knowledge. Thank you for encouraging me to write a personal manifesto. You are an inspiring example of what it means to be a good person, teacher, Christian, and friend.

Tracy Walder, my first Model UN advisor. Thank you for everything you have given me, from awarding me opportunity to serve your Model UN club in a leadership position, to livening my spirits when time away from home became unbearable. I am still sorry that you had to come downstairs in your pajamas when I was seven minutes late for curfew; it will not happen again. I am so glad to have met you.

Dr. Chris Hamel, my independent study advisor. You were the first teacher I met at Heritage Hall, and proved my first staunch advocate. Through all the mini-disasters, meetings, and conferences, you remained optimistic and confident in my mission. Thank you for betting on a new student with a complicated, challenging, and time-consuming project. I will forever appreciate your encouragement and assurance. Thank you for believing in me.

The high school and middle school Heritage Hall Model UN club members. First of all, thank you for signing up for the club. I had such an amazing time attending conferences with you. You guys made my Model UN experience better than I could have ever hoped.

Mr. Guy Bramble, Mr. Keith Cassell, and Mr. Ron Allie. Thank you for allowing me to bring Model UN to Heritage Hall. You are the most supportive and accommodating administrators I have ever had the pleasure of knowing. I am so blessed to have found Heritage Hall; I am just sorry I did not discover your enviable institution earlier in my high school career.

The UNA-OKC chapter. Thank you for your unrelenting assistance and backing. The work you do in our community is spectacular. Thank you for spreading the United Nations' mission with the great state of Oklahoma.

Bill Bryant, for sharing your knowledge of the United Nations. Thank you for agreeing to speak at my annual conference, and for contributing to this book. You are the most kind-hearted, trustworthy man I have ever met.

Jarrett Jobe. Thank you for agreeing to speak at my annual conference. Your passion for international relations, the United Nations, and the subject for nuclear disarmament are contagious. Never stop bringing interesting, engaging exchange students to Oklahoma City.

Vicki Gourley, for allowing me to write countless articles about Model UN in your spectacular paper. Thank you for providing me the opportunity to share my passion through such an inclusive medium.

I could not, and will not, attempt to thank every person who has inspired and influenced me throughout my years, so I will conclude with a blanket expression of gratitude. Thank you to everyone in my life; family, friends, and teachers. You have all played a critical role in my development, and your influence and support has made me the person I am today.

Bibliography

"Home." *Harvard National Model United Nations*. N.p., n.d. Web.

"Delegate Guide." *Harvard National Model United Nations*. 2014. Print.

"United Nations Association." *Association of the USA*. N.p., n.d. Web.

"Best Delegate." *Best Delegate RSS*. N.p., n.d. Web.

Mickolus, Edward F., and J. Thomas Brannan. *Coaching Winning Model United Nations Teams: A Teacher's Guide*. Dulles, VA: Potomac, 2013. Print.

Charter of the United Nations. Washington: U.S. Govt. Print. Off., 1945. Print.

"Michigan State University Model United Nations." *Michigan State University Model United Nations*. N.p., 19 Mar. 2012. Web.

National Model United Nations Delegate Preparation Guide (n.d.): n. pag. *National Model United Nations*. 2013. Web.

"The National Model United Nations Rules of Procedure." *National Model United Nations*. N.p., n.d. Web. 27 June 2015.

"Guide to Model UN Procedure." *The Ivy League Model United Nations Conference 2014*. N.p., 2014.

"Guide to Writing Resolutions." *The Ivy League Model United Nations Conference 2014*. N.p., 2014. Web.

"Guide to Writing Position Papers" *The Ivy League Model United Nations Conference 2014*. N.p., 2014. Web.

"Delegates | United Nations." *UN News Center*. UN, n.d. Web.

"The William & Mary International Relations Club Guide to Model United Nations." *William & Mary*. N.p., n.d. Web.

"Model United Nations of the Southwest Conference Guide." *Model United Nations of the Southwest*. The University of Oklahoma Precollegiate Programs, Print.

VIVIAN ARMITAGE

<u>NOTES</u>

<u>NOTES</u>

<u>NOTES</u>

Made in the USA
Lexington, KY
16 August 2016